The Unspoken Formula *to* Fast Fortunes

Know & Grow Rich

Jamie L. Briggs

Cover Design: Derek Chiodo @ www.eCoverMakers.com

Royalty Free Stock Photos: Fotolia

Editor: Nalani M. Briggs

Contact Author:

Jamie L. Briggs

P.O. Box 602

Farmingville, NY 11738

www.JamieLBriggs.com

The Unspoken Formula to Fast Fortunes: Know & Grow Rich

ISBN 978-0-578-03341-9

1. Finance, Personal   2. Self-Help Techniques

Printed in the United States of America

Table of Contents

Introduction

Now unto him that is able to do exceeding abundantly above all
that we ask or think, according to the power that worketh in us.
~ Ephesians 3:20 ~

If the scripture above didn't get you extremely excited, the first time around, then I ask that you take this time to re-read it again. On second thought, read it again, anyway, for reinforcement purposes because the entire topic of this book is about that wondrous yet unknown power that "worketh in us". Let me make it completely clear, from the very beginning of this book, that even though time-tested scriptures will be referenced, along with legendary sayings and powerful quotes, *this revolutionary information has nothing to do with religion.* In fact, **all faiths are acceptable, when reading this book, though possessing no set faith is just as fine**. The bottom line is: Regardless of your background or prior path, you were destined to read a book, as resourceful as this one, because we were all born to live the most magical life, imaginable.

All throughout this book, undeniable proof will be provided that an omnipresent power does exist, and will be pin-pointed to inside of ourselves as opposed to outside of ourselves, as we were taught to believe, in our youth. There *is* a power that *is* "able to do **exceeding abundantly above all that we ask or think**" and the greatest news of all is that this "power, worketh in us". After reading this book, in its entirety, you will not only be officially introduced and informed, to the fullest extent, about this omnipotent force but you will be taught, for the first time, exactly how to tap into this power, without fail.

You can be confident that any and all obstacles, which once stood in your way, will not only be addressed but easily overcome, throughout the book. Step-by-step, we will also uncover the unknown formula for fast fortunes and discover how to harvest any outcome you crave, on command, in the fastest, most pleasurable time frame possible. How do I know that this formula is achievable, believable and fail-proof? Because I have been actively applying it, since the age of 18, and I always receive the astonishing end result I expect, every time. "The Unspoken Formula to Fast Fortunes" is fine-tuned and tested, for over 10 years, which makes me well-equipped to explain this extraordinary process, with the highest precision. All throughout this book, I will also be sharing a few of my most captivating stories of manifestation to further assist you in retaining the formula and to strengthen the support of this material.

No stone will be left unturned and by the end of this book I can assure you the acceleration you seek. You will find that your life will have been significantly enhanced for having read this book, from start to finish, and your newly attained knowledge will take you to the next level, whether you choose to act on this information or not. With that being said, know that there is no pressure on your part, as you allow me, the author, to do my work, which is not only to entertain you but enlighten you, at your perfect pace.

Everything will be explained to you, in order of importance, and spoken in a very straightforward style. There are millions of books on the market about Manifesting, Quantum Physics, and The Law of Attraction that are more suitable for physicists, like Albert Einstein, or scientists, such as Sir Isaac Newton, because they leave their loyal reader without an easy-to-understand plan for achieving repeatable results.

I have read over 2,000 of these types of books, which have always left me more optimistic than before, but none of them delivered me the message I needed, to yield quick and real results. I came to the conclusion that they spend too much time, focusing on technicalities of function that don't make much sense to the unscientific type thinker, while failing to divulge the appropriate amount of time towards teaching the specific steps that do work, regardless of the person applying them. Almost all of these books also fail to permanently impart the necessary feelings of exhilaration and expectancy that their readers so richly deserve.

Let me prepare you for the simple system that you are about to fall in love with and can turn to, whenever you desire to bring forth good fortune, in *any and all areas of your life*. We all know how to turn on a light bulb, by simply flipping a switch, and that if we dial any 7 or 11 digit combination, on our telephone key pad that the call will go through as we had hoped. We also know that when we turn the key in the ignition, our well-kept vehicle is going to start. And last but not least, the moment we click the cable button on our remote control, we do not doubt that our television is going to turn on. Do any of these tasks seem difficult to you or require strenuous faith for results? They most definitely do not, so therefore, the answer is an unequivocal "No".

Excellent! Now you are starting to see that everything is really supposed to be as simple as "flipping a switch" and "turning a key". The challenges and obstacles only come into play when we waste our precious time, trying to figure out or fret over the "does it really matter" details. Do you really need to know how to manufacture a microwave or do you genuinely desire a hot meal, in less than 5 minutes? Let the scientists solve the mysteries and establish the systems but at least grant yourself, the permission to simply plug in, immediately, for the most enjoyable experiences.

I am one of the few authors that is not going to trivialize your time or mind, with the complicated components of manifesting your designated desires, but will plainly show you how to manifest pleasing amounts of money and any other good fortune you desire, as easily as an office manager would train an administrative assistant, on how to send a fax. Do you really want to know or worry yourself with the scientific steps it takes, that causes a fax to transmit, or do you prefer to focus on the outcome you desire, which is having your fax sent to its intended destination, within seconds? Ask yourself this: Do you really need to know those perplexing processes or do you agree with me that such things are a waste of your time and energies, which could be better utilized, elsewhere.

I applaud you for being willing to abandon those ways that don't work or take too long to learn, and for being open to trying an innovative application that operates at a rapid rate. You are about to embark on a journey that transforms "desiring" into "acquiring" and while on this personal adventure, you will have no internal struggle, temporarily setting aside the things that are important to everyone else. The time has arrived where **YOU** are going to begin, believing in yourself, like never before and start tapping into the power, within, for manifesting **YOUR** fondest dreams, with a confidential formula that always acts fast.

Warmest welcome to the forgotten realm where fortunes reign and riches rule!!!

Jamie Lynn Briggs

father finally started to get mad after about the fifth time some stranger knocked on our front door, inquiring about the price, so I stopped trying to sell that "hunk of junk". We never had any cool cars and that is what fueled my desire to make my first one, something special.

I walked right up to my father, while he was washing the rusty old Nova, and I told him, with complete confidence, that when I got my license, that green Dodge Shadow convertible was the very vehicle I was going to be driving. I meant what I said, the minute those words came out of my mouth, and I never considered another car for the next 2 years.

The day I turned 18, I scheduled my road test and I passed, on the first try. Within one hour of receiving my temporary paper license, I stopped at all the stores that I could think of, that carried the Auto Mart Magazines, trying to track down my 1994 Dodge Shadow convertible. I didn't care how many calls I had to make because in my mind, that car was mine, no matter what I had to do.

I was not worried in the least bit when the first twenty places I called, told me that there was no way I was going to locate that exact car. One salesman told me that the 1994 Dodge Shadow was a demo of some sort and that only 500, in total, were manufactured. I never took the time to research if what he told me was true because nothing was going to stop me from getting what I wanted anyway. Another sales person said that I would have better luck, trying to find a needle in a haystack, while several other sellers tried to talk me into getting a LeBaron convertible instead, because they were the most popular, that year. Everyone else I spoke with, that did not carry my dream car, told me that I was being way too specific with the make, model, year and color.

I wasn't going to let anyone change my mind or talk me into any other options. I KNEW what I wanted and I KNEW I would get it.

After I spent 3 nights of making countless phone calls, contacting every single dealership in my state, none of them knew where I could claim my car. Did this make me worried? Not for a second! The next step that I needed to take had already popped into my mind.

My parents had moved to the sunshine state of Florida that previous year and I thought to myself…"CONVERTIBLE CAPITAL". I quickly called my father and I asked him if he could call around, about MY 1994 Dodge Shadow convertible, emphasizing that it MUST be green, with a cream-colored top. I told him I would touch base, in a few days. In the meantime, I spent the next few nights, calling all of the dealerships in the surrounding states of New York, but to no avail. When I followed up with my father, he was sad to say that he had no luck either, in locating the car.

One week went by, since I obtained my license, and I couldn't come up with another way to acquisition my dream car. But, I still had no doubts that I would make my purchase, any day now. That same evening, my boyfriend's father informed me that his boss was selling a "never been owned before", 1996 Chevy Cavalier. I had actually wanted a teal-colored Chevy Cavalier, before getting a glimpse of the gorgeous green Dodge Shadow convertible. Although I had my heart set on getting the 1994 Dodge Shadow convertible, doing everything in my personal power to find this car but having no luck, I agreed to take a look at the Cavalier, considering I once wanted that kind of car, too. I "tossed and turned" all night because **I knew,** deep down, that I **was not** going to desire the Cavalier over the Shadow.

The next day, we went to go look at the 1996 Chevy Cavalier. In spite of this car being brand new and painted the prettiest color pink, I suddenly found myself with severe stomach pains that I had never felt before. My mid section hurt so bad that I made my boyfriend's father, rush me right home. No negotiations were to take place that day. My stomach pains continued, throughout the car ride home, but they stopped, within minutes of walking through the front door. Even though my stomach pains were now gone, I started to feel "bummed out", not knowing how to get my hands on my "phantom" fantasy car.

When my boyfriend arrived home from work, he could see I was upset and he asked if there was anything that would make me feel better. Oddly, I was craving pizza all afternoon so he took me to the pizza parlor, around the corner. After we finished eating, and exited the pizza place, we walked towards his truck and my eyes instantly gravitated towards a pink-colored car in the parking lot. This car was the same color as the Cavalier I had seen, earlier that day, and while it had the same body style as the Shadow, it was not a convertible. All of a sudden, I felt a freaky kick in the middle of my stomach and **I JUST KNEW** what I needed to do.

I insisted to my boyfriend that I leave our telephone number on the windshield but he advised against it. There was no way I wasn't going to act, after my gut kicked the way it did, so I wrote down my work number, without hesitation. When I returned to the office, on Monday morning, I got a phone call from a pleasant speaking woman who introduced herself as Barbara, asking to speak with me. I informed her that for some strange reason, I was very drawn to her car and I inquired if she would be willing to sell it, if the price was right. The way I saw it, at the time, was that if I couldn't get a grip on my 1994 Dodge Shadow convertible, then at least **I, and no one else, would be the one** to declare "who" the "runner up" would be.

Barbara was so sweet to even put through the call to me because she shared with me that her daughter just got her license also and would be giving her the car as a gift. I thanked her for making me aware of her plans and I asked her to hold onto my phone number in case she changed her mind. That was the extent of our two minute conversation.

The next day proved uneventful but then on Wednesday evening, my boyfriend's father asked me if I had any intentions of buying the Cavalier from his boss. I forgot all about the Chevy and I was told that his boss had been holding it for me. His boss wanted $6K but he offered to sell it to me for $5K because of my "family" connection and not knowing what else to do, I told him that I would stop by, on Saturday, to take the car "off of his hands".

What else was I supposed to do, I reasoned with my self? I did everything I could think of and frankly, I was out of ideas. I had made over a hundred phone calls; looked at another vehicle when I wasn't the least bit interested, and I left my work number on some stranger's car, off of a strong hunch. Little did I realize, at the time, was that **I did do everything right** and that all of the pieces were falling perfectly into place!

As I fell asleep that evening, I recall crying out to the heavens, in one last desperate attempt to affirm that I truly desired the Dodge Shadow, that if some stroke of luck didn't come through in the next three days, then I would faithfully fulfill my promise to purchase the Cavalier. This plead was a pivotal moment for me because I finally released my intense feelings about the Dodge Shadow and even though I still desired it dearly, I no longer felt frantic.

I coasted through the next day, without thinking anything of it. Before I knew it, it was Friday morning and I prepared myself that come Saturday, I would be putting my money down on a 1996 Chevy Cavalier the day thereafter. *Are you asking yourself if I was happy about what was to come?* The honest answer is that I didn't feel too much of anything, that day, and I was basically just going through the motions of that moment.

Quitting time finally arrived at 5:00pm and I carried out my regular routine in "closing down shop". Then, out of the blue, the phone rang, and as tempted as I was to let the answering machine take care of the caller, I felt prompted to pick up the telephone. The caller requested to speak with me and when I asked, "Who's calling"?, she replied, "Barbara". I immediately realized that this was the woman whose vehicle I left my work number on, when at the pizza place, the previous weekend. I was definitely happy and hopeful, when I heard her voice and I anxiously asked if she had changed her mind about selling her car. She compassionately communicated that her decision still stood about giving her car to her daughter but that she had spotted a car, out of the corner of her eye, while heading home from work that she thought I might like.

Keep in mind that I am only 18 at the time, as I immaturely think to myself, "How on earth does this woman think she knows what I want when she doesn't even know me and has never met me"?

In an attempt to mask my attitude, I amused her and I asked what it was that she "spotted", that made her think of me. Without picking up on my apprehension, she answered back, with enthusiasm in her voice," A dark green Dodge Shadow convertible with a cream-colored top". I went into "instant shock mode", my hands started to tremble, and then the receiver of the phone fell from my ear, onto the floor.

When I returned to my senses and I retrieved the receiver from the floor, I urgently asked Barbara to tell me the exact location of that car. I scrambled to find a pen, to write down the directions. I was caught completely off-guard and I was so overwhelmed by what had just happened that I never got to tell Barbara how this was the car I had been wanting since I was 16. But fortunately, just before I hung up the phone with her, I blurted out, "You are a part of a major miracle"! I bolted out of the office like lightning and I told my friend who was waiting outside for me to "put the petal to the metal".

As soon as my boyfriend pulled into the driveway, I wouldn't even let him get out of the car and made him take me to the town where Barbara had spotted my dream car. We drove up and down that busy road, during rush hour traffic, but could not find the Auto Body shop that Barbara had mentioned. After 45 minutes of circling the same section, we were starting to get frustrated and we thought that maybe my sister had someone play a prank on me because we "mess around a lot" like that. Then, as we were turning around to head home, I started clapping my hands uncontrollably, because right in front of where we u-turned was the Auto Body shop that Barbara referenced.

We ripped right into a parking lot but we did not see a dark green Dodge Shadow convertible, anywhere. As we walked along the side of the building, my eyes lit up like never before because 5 feet in front of me was my dream car with a reassuring "For Sale" sign on the windshield. "Oh, thank God"!!, I said, out loud, with such a sigh of relief. It would be one thing to track down the Dodge but I would have been frustrated, beyond words, if it was not for sale. I couldn't help but walk around the car, at least a dozen times, and as luck would have it, there was not a single scratch or stain on this car.

We did not have cell phones back then so as soon as we got home, I called the number on the "For Sale" sign. Mileage didn't matter to me or anything else for that matter so I came right out and asked the seller how much he wanted for the car. I already had access to the $5,000.00 that I was going to be using, to buy the Cavalier the next day, but to my surprise, he said, "$3,500.00". **Is that not just too good to be true?!** I was going to get the car of my dreams, just in the nick of time, and I was spending less then I was willing to for a car I didn't really want. **Does it get better then that?!!**

Needless to say, I went back the next day and I drove my dream car, home. My friends and family got as much joy out of that car as I did. Not a weekend went by where I didn't wax that car and clean the carpets. For the next 4 years, I loved every second that I owned that car and never once did it have a single mechanical problem. I never needed to rotate the tires or replace the brakes, like most cars would require. All I had to do was "fill her up" with gas and get my maintenance oil changes.

The day finally came, when I had my sights set on another new vehicle, so I advertised the Dodge Shadow in our local circular. I would not sell my miraculous convertible to just anyone, refusing 3 excellent offers, because I needed to know that this car was not going to get taken for granted. I actually accepted a lower offer, over the others, because the man I decided to sell to, told me he wanted this car more then any thing else he had come across and I **just sensed** that he would appreciate this vehicle as much as I did.

In the next chapter, we are going to get to the bottom of *how* this truly miraculous event, from my teenage years, happened **and** *how* you, too, can tap into this force, **whenever you want for whatever you want**, but first, let me point out 3 exciting facts, to realistically raise up your expectancy level.

First, within 2 fast weeks, I became the proud new owner of the 1994 Dodge Shadow convertible, green with a cream-colored top, which was precisely what I wanted.

Let me also emphasize that 2 weeks is **not** a long time at all, to hold out for what you really want, and that most of the time, manifesting what you want can happen much quicker, when you know exactly what you are doing. Also, do not allow a single soul to talk you out of what **you truly want;** cease from settling for second best because it is never necessary.

Next, notice that everything unfolded exactly as it was supposed to, and in a most magnificent manner. It was not only exhilarating that I got the car of my dreams, but the hunch that led me to the woman who located my car for me is an astonishing story that I continue to amaze other people with and will continue to amaze, for many more decades to come. Also, when you passionately act on the intuitive ideas that come to you and let go of the impulse to act when the ideas aren't arriving, that is when you can almost certainly expect that your desire is about to be delivered.

Last but not least, do not concern yourself with time or demand a determined amount of days for your dream to come true. Most often when we do this, we actually postpone what could have come quite quickly if we didn't project it into the distant future. It is an absolute misconception and myth that some desires may take months or years to manifest. All dreams and desires are able to be made manifest the moment any individual makes up their own mind that they are ready, right then, to receive what they want. The initial inception starts the very same instant any individual insists on manifesting something specific.

Also, isn't it ironic that my Dodge Shadow appeared to me the day before I was going to buy the Chevy Cavalier and not the day after? I can assure you that when your mind is made up about going for what you want, it will never be a day over due.

We are just beginning to scratch the surface of what we can manifest and how little time it takes to turn dreams into reality so let's move on to Chapter 2 where will we pin-point the power that makes these things possible...

Locating and Activating Your Total Personal Power

Magic is believing in yourself. If you can do that you can make
anything happen.
~ Johann Wolfgang von Goethe (1749-1832) ~

The wisest man to ever walk the earth could sit beside you
and utter all the mysteries of the Universe in your ear but it would
be worthless if you are filled with fear or deep seated self-doubt.
Fear and doubt would have you dismiss any accurate information
that came your way or cause you to claim that you are not good
enough to engage in such a powerful process. This chapter is
designed to remove most of your self-doubt and permanently
replace it with radical self-belief. We will rip *fear*, out at the roots, in
Chapter 9.

Those persons, who whole-heartedly believe in themselves,
do in fact, make magical experiences manifest and they can accomplish anything that they desire, with next-to-no effort. It is the
easiest thing in the world, to establish a sturdy belief in yourself,
when you are aware of what has been holding you back and you
resolve to remove those blocks from your life. By the end of this
book, your self-belief is going to skyrocket and you will be rip-
roaring ready to turn dreams into reality with "The Unspoken
Formula to Fast Fortunes".

Self-belief is the foundation for all fortunes, luck and wealth.
It is almost impossible for the average person to experience any
degree of wealth because they unknowingly give all their power
away, every day. All the self-made wealthy people of this world
have learnt how to take back and tap into their total personal power.
You can activate your personal power as soon as you can locate
where it is has been hiding.

Do you not see it, in the eyes of almost everyone you come into contact with, their sad demeanor of defeat? You see 1 smile for every 10 frowns. The reason for all this anguish is because people feel powerless. The one way to overcome this problem is by repeatedly reminding people of their innate personal power, however, throughout this entire book we will be fully focusing on only YOU. It is YOUR time to prosper, like those that have before you, because you are determined to discover what it takes to do so.

Our total personal power resides right here, in the present moment, and it always will. Our minds have formed the habit of constantly looking back to past disappointing experiences and frequently foreseeing potential future failures. The "good old days" and the "drudged old days" ARE over. You got through them or got to enjoy every second of them, whatever the case may be, and the power within you to manifest nice, new experiences is at hand right now, regardless of what you may have already witnessed or how much you have aged. Your total personal power is yours to use, whenever you want for whatever you want, until the day you depart from this planet.

I am going to let you in on one of life's little secret so do not take it lightly. Think it through as many times as it takes for it to make sense...

The projector is responsible for the picture that appears on the screen. YOU are the projector. The world is the screen. You have the power and permission to change the reality being reflected, in any instant, if you so desire. If images of lack and struggle are all over the screen, simply insert the disc, with all the images of the wealth you want.

You may not be ready to completely comprehend or accept this fact, for the moment, but as we progress it *will* all come together perfectly for you, like a picture from out of several puzzle pieces.

Now that we are starting to accept that we can not beg back or buy back our past and we are awakening to the truth that all power to produce, resides in the present moment. We must also acknowledge that we have been pushing our dreams off to a distant place in the future or hoping that, one day down the road, things will work out on their own. Since it is a proven fact that people retain things that rhyme much more effectively than things that don't, I created a home-run-hitting poem to get my message across adequately...

YOUR Body is right here...right NOW
YOUR Mind and Spirit too,
They did NOT stay in yesterday, so why on earth would YOU?

Tomorrow can NOT even come
Until TODAY is through,
The future doesn't dare compare to the power within YOU!

There is NO greater moment
Then THIS ONE that you ARE IN,
The REST of your life is the BEST of your life so shall we not begin...

You forfeit all your total personal power when you permit yourself to get lost in thoughts about the past and fantasize or fear over the future. We will uncover within these pages how to get your body, mind and spirit centered in the present moment for maximum results. You are comprised of these 3 aspects and would cease to function as a human being if any one of them were missing so it makes perfect sense to align all that you are, in the perfect point of power, for anything that your heart desires.

Now would be a wonderful time to share another one of my true manifestation stories with you to prove that magic abounds for the person who believes in themselves and how creating anything you crave on conscious command is possible when you are perfectly aligned in your present point of power. In the next chapter, we will expose the exclusive six steps for manifesting all of your dearest dreams and desires. I have come to call this "The Free Cup of Coffee Story"…

I had rented a movie from the video store that I forgotten all about and knew it was going to be about a week late. I asked my boyfriend to take a ride with me and told him that I would drop it in the return box outside then I'd pay the late fee, next time. The video store was only 3 blocks from where we lived and since we planned on returning right home, we just jumped in the truck, without grabbing our wallets.

When I got back into the truck after doing the drop, I had a strong desire for a cup of coffee. I was well aware that neither of us were carrying any cash but that didn't make me stop desiring a hot cup of coffee. I expressed my desire to my boyfriend by specifically saying out loud, "I want a free cup of coffee". He immediately reminded me that we didn't bring our money and then I informed him that that was why I said "I want a FREE cup of coffee". My boyfriend was always great about going along with my whims and actually entertained my idea for a free cup of coffee.

I thought of a place where we could both get our coffees for free. A good friend of mine worked at Starbucks at the time and I would have her "hook us up", then I'd pay her back, the next time we got together. I ran it by my boyfriend and he headed straight to Starbucks. When we arrived, I did not see my friend inside the store or her car in the parking lot so, we figured she wasn't working that night.

My boyfriend felt bad and he asked me where else could we go, for a free cup of coffee. I thought it was so cool of him to carry on the catch phrase, "free cup of coffee", and rather than be disappointed, we both busted out laughing. We decided to take a different way home, than the way we took there, and while we were driving, I said out loud, one last time, "I still want a free cup of coffee". The second I stopped speaking, a crystal clear image of a truck stop and shop, instantly flashed into my mind. I have never experienced this instant intuitive flash phenomenon before and I quickly told my boyfriend what had just happened. The truck stop that popped into my mind would be coming up on the road we were on and although neither of us had ever been there before, I knew exactly where it was.

As we were approaching the light where the truck stop and shop was, I urged my boyfriend to make a right turn into the parking lot. Without hesitation, we went inside and started making our coffees. While I was mixing the milk and sugar in the cup, my boyfriend looked up at me, skeptically, as if to say, "What do we think we are doing"? He could see from my facial expression that I was certain everything was going to work out so we put the lids, over our fresh cups of coffee, and proceeded to the cash register.

There were 2 people ahead of us and while they were getting rung up, I didn't have a worry in the world but I can't say the same about my boyfriend. We got called up by the clerk after the person in front of us was finished paying. Once we approached the counter, the clerk looked at me and said, "Those coffees are on me". I shot him back the biggest smile! In disbelief and shock, my boyfriend asked the clerk to repeat what he just said. The clerk came right back with, "Those coffees are for FREE; they are on me, so go on and have a nice night". We both thanked the clerk, then we got back into the truck. My boyfriend just sat there, stunned for a few minutes, while I sipped my coffee and giggled.

You must admit, that this manifestation was pretty miraculous? A free cup of coffee might not be on anyone's wish list but the formula for making things like that happen, consistently, should be every person's primary priority. You too will be able to create any amazing outcome you aspire to as soon as we get you appropriately aligned.

In order to get you accurately adjusted and aligned, we will need to overcome a common problem that haunts the minds of most people and then we can assure a "clean slate, to create like crazy".

There is not a single soul alive that has not said or done several things that they are not proud of. Do you beat yourself up repeatedly for things that you did years ago? Would you pass judgment on your best friend if they admitted to making the same mistakes that you did? We are so quick to tear ourselves apart for all of our shortcomings but we wouldn't dare say such horrific things to our best friend's face that we think about ourselves, in the silent recesses of our own minds.

When people *know* better they *do* better. The truth is: <u>Hurt</u> people, hurt <u>people</u>. However, what you **really** need to know is that **nobody has the power to hurt you, without your permission.** Simply distance yourself from those people that repeatedly drag down your spirits. You have done not-so-nice things at one time or another and other people have done not-so-nice things to you. No one is exempt from this double-sided scenario.

You do not need to waste your time seeking forgiveness from those that have hurt you when you have the power at your disposal to fully forgive yourself.

There are a lot of people who were abused as children, by adults who they themselves, were abused as children but the cycle stops when **you** say so. We have all been beaten down by one thing or another, at some point in life, to bring us to the ultimate level of the most personal power, which is unconditional love of ourselves. Bad things have happened to all of us and we have done some bad things as well but none of those things make us less lovable or banned from tapping into our total personal power whenever we are ready to release our past.

Those persons, who believe in themselves, forgive themselves as fast as they would a best friend, for any wrong doing. Those persons, who believe in themselves, have freed themselves from the grips of guilt by being thankful for the new day, before them. They commit to making the most of the new day by doing things different than the day before. Those persons, who believe in themselves, need no apologies for past afflictions and correct their own course, whenever possible, by burying things in the past, where they belong.

If you can not forgive yourself for something that you did, that may have deeply hurt someone, then chances are that someone did something to you that hurt hard core. Your forgiveness was ready to be received, the day the damage was done, and same holds true, for your offender. Forgiveness is a gift that we give to ourselves and we need not seek it from another person but we are responsible to receive it for ourselves. Worry not about anybody else being forgiven for they will request it, in their right time, but concern yourself with absolving anything that you regretfully did wrong.

Behold, now is the accepted time: behold, now is the day of salvation.
~ 2 Corinthians 6:2 ~

Today is the day, you can deem yourself fully forgiven for any mistakes you may have made and move on, with your head held high for favorable fresh outcomes. You can't reverse time nor should you want to when the power to turn it all around is right now.

If on the other hand, you thought that the good old days were as great as they get then you've got another thing coming to you. We are going to get you excited, about the year ahead, with a proven formula for intentionally calling forth all the things that will make this your best year yet.

If your current conditions find you in a place of poor health, frugal finances or lacking luck in relationships then this is the most opportune time for us to pin-point your personal power and assert to activate it at once.

Your total person power is only accessible in the very same spot you now sit or stand. Remember this rhyme…"Now is how so stay in the day". You have no need to turn back to "days gone by" to figure out what you want most, to manifest from this moment forward. You can not count on the future to deliver your dreams if you do not decree, in this day, what those dreams are to be. Therefore, it is transparently clear that your total personal power is based in your dexterity to make definite decisions in the present and remain devoted to those decisions until the moment they manifest.

All throughout this book we will be proving the power of making split second definite decisions along with determining the months ahead by pre-picking what we would have happen. We are no longer going to keep our fingers crossed, hope, pray or wish our days away and remain miserable. From now on, we are going to confidently custom create all the good fortune we long for and courageously tap into our personal power even if everyone else around us chooses to stay stuck.

Most human beings don't dare tap into their total personal power for fear of not fitting in or feeling bad for those, less fortunate. We think that if we worry about everyone else and dwell on the bad things that are happening all around the world, that it makes us a good person or somehow helps matters. You are a good person, period, and the truth is that you can not contribute to the welfare of the world or the lives of those you love until you learn how to tap into your total personal power. There is no limit to what you will be able to accomplish for yourself and others when you unleash "The Unspoken Formula to Fast Fortunes".

We will move on in just a moment but before we do, might I remind you...

Now unto him that is able to do exceeding abundantly above all that we ask or think, according to the power that worketh in us.
~ Ephesians 3:20 ~

The invisible force that infinitely oversees our Universe and keeps the cosmos under constant control is able to do exceedingly abundantly above all we ask or think, every time we exercise our birthright to make definite decisions that are based on receiving our heart's desires. It clearly states that the power worketh in us but we have been taught to believe that the power is outside of ourselves and has no interest in human heart desires. *Where* do you think the desires of our hearts stem from and *why* do you think it is that we all have our own unique set of desires?

As soon as we stop searching the ends of the earth, surfing the internet and putting all of our faith into other people, we will then come into possession of our total personal power. When we stop focusing on outside sources and start listening to the whispers within, we can then uncover what worthy dreams to apply our power towards obtaining faster then we ever thought possible.

Let's sum up this chapter by breaking down the important points from "The Free Cup of Coffee Story" and then we can forge into the formula.

Notice how I did not deny my desire for a cup of coffee. I immediately accepted and honored my heart's desire, by simply stating what I wanted, without any attachment. I was extremely specific about what I wanted and I affirmed that it had to be free since I had no money on hand. I believed in myself enough to make my desire, manifest. I did not worry about how my desire would unfold but maintained total trust, the entire time. In a matter of minutes, my inner guidance informed me on what I needed to do to manifest my desire. I went with my intuition and everything worked out wonderfully, just as I had expected.

Intuition is not reserved for a select few and it is available to all who are wise enough to know that it exists within everyone. Your intuition will ignite, every time you make a definite decision, and it will undeniably direct you to your dreams.

Vow now to believe in yourself more then you do anyone else alive and watch how quickly you are able to transform your world. Everyone else will believe in you too when they see how much you believe in yourself. In return, you will inspire them to believe in themselves as well. Establishing an unbreakable belief in yourself, is the most personal, most priceless *and* the most valuable gift you could give to the world.

The Unspoken Formula to Fast Fortunes

What lies behind us and what lies ahead of us are tiny matter
compared to what lies within us.
~ Ralph Waldo Emerson (1803-1882) ~

We have already made some substantial progress and you
are starting to become comfortable with the concept that a very real
power resides inside of you so without further delay why don't we
dive right into the formula?

**The Six Simple & Straightforward Exclusive Steps for
Fortunes:**

1. *KNOW* that **you** *CAN* have *ANYTHING* your heart desires.
2. *Describe every detail* of your desire, out loud or on paper.
3. *Make up your mind* that you *WILL* get what you want.
4. *Fine tune your feelings* by establishing a state of certainty.
5. *Follow all actions* you are gravitated towards.
6. *Take over ownership* of your heart's desire.

If I were you, I would grab a new notebook now and hand-
write these simple six steps as they appear above. By putting pen to
paper you command your mind to pay attention and absorb all the
new information you are adamant about retaining. These are the
explicit six steps I employ, every time, I want to manifest my
dreams into physical reality. They are all as simple as they seem and
we will get your mind to master them in no time.

Time to share another true story that revolves around these steps and then we will break them down, bit by bit.

With these extremely simple 6 steps, I was not only able to magically manifest (1) expensive Movado watch but (2) Movado watches, within 1 week of each other.

When I was working for a sales company in Commack that I will tell you more about in Chapter 7, I couldn't help but notice that almost everyone I worked with was wearing a Movado watch. I could care less about owning a fancy watch before working at this place but the more I saw them, the more I wanted one. I didn't force myself to want a Movado watch, I just naturally started to desire one of my own. The day I made up my mind that I really did want a Movado of my own, I wrote it down in my notebook. At this point, I didn't know the details to the watch I wanted but I did KNOW, specifically, that it was a Movado.

That weekend, my 2 close friends and I spontaneously decided to spend the day at the Outlets. When we walked out of one of the fragrance stores, I instantly spotted a Movado sign and asked my friends if they would wait for me while I took a look. I knew I wanted a Movado but I didn't know the design I desired. The only way to figure that out would be by trying on a few, inside the store. I tried on approximately 10 watches before definitely deciding on the one I wanted the most. The watch I wanted was priced at a little over $1K and I had the sales lady write down the model number for me on the back of her business card. The dollar amount didn't matter to me that day because my goal was to figure out exactly what I wanted then let the watch manifest on my wrist whatever way it may.

When we got home that evening from shopping at the Outlets, I pulled my notebook back out and wrote down the details about the watch I wanted. I specified that the wrist band must be gold and the face plate be black, with its trademark signature diamond spec on the top.

When I returned to work after having the weekend off, I was instantly inspired when I saw a Movado watch box in the lunchroom garbage can. The person who does not know the 6 simple steps to manifesting, like I did at the time, would have become bitter or annoyed that someone else apparently got what they wanted. The novice's inability to identify the empty Movado box, as being a sign that his/her desire was well on the way, would instead, end up being the un-fine-tuned feelings, blocking his/her desire from ever unfolding. On the flip side of the same coin, fine-tuned feelings, centered in certainty, mandates our desire to manifest now.

After seeing that empty Movado box, it was settled inside of me that I *would* get my gold and black Movado, without a shadow of a doubt. My cousin invited me and my family over for brunch, that upcoming Saturday. My sister Jennifer, who was sitting diagonally from me, at the table, told me that she had something to give me. I was a little surprised because although we were close at one point in our lives, my sister and I had grown apart. I was curious to see what she got for me and I didn't think to wait for everyone to finish their meals before asking outright what it was.

My sister pulled out a beautifully wrapped box, from her pocketbook, which she then handed to me. I slowly removed the wrapping paper and the onyx black box, underneath, boldly revealed the silver foiled Movado name, on the outside. I must have looked like a monkey, busting into a banana, to my family members when they witnessed me ferociously flip open the top of the box. I naturally nodded my head back and forth, with a major smirk on my face, when I discovered the watch inside the box. It was the exact one I had written down in my notebook…"Gold band with a black face plate and its trademark signature diamond spec on the top". Of course, I showed my sister the business card from the weekend earlier, and thanked her profusely. My whole family was overjoyed from this experience.

Is that not wild or what?!! But wait…it gets even better because I desired a different Movado watch, the following week.

The watch my sister gave me was great and I couldn't be happier about getting it as a gift. I wore it to work every day that week and showed it off to all my Movado-admiring co-workers. I am anal when it comes to making sure all my accessories perfectly match my attire and the gold watch with the black face didn't go with some of my outfits. I pulled out my nifty notebook once more, as I jotted down: "silver band with a white face but must be Movado".

Within one week of writing down my new Movado watch specifications, the perfect process for me to receive my desire unfolded yet again *and* even more miraculous than the first time.

I was the passenger in my friend Melissa's car, while driving on the highway, back to my place. I impulsively asked her to get onto the service road so we could stop at the upcoming 7-11 for a drink, before she dropped me off. While I was standing beside my friend, who was making herself a cup of coffee, this crazy looking man approached me. He pointed to my wrist and asked if I wanted another Movado watch. The man may have been spooky but he certainly had my attention, after mentioning "Movado". I answered back that the only way I would want another one is if it was silver with a white face. This mad man began to chuckle in front of me and my friend because that was exactly what he had. As we stepped outside, he lifted up the lid of the box, displaying my latest desire. The original price tag was attached to the watch, valued at $799.99. I asked him how much he wanted and he quickly declared, "$100.00". I'm a sharp shooter myself so I answered back, just as fast, that I would give him two twenties and a ten. I offered him half of what he was asking and he jumped all over it. I had no problem paying $50.00 for the $800.00 watch I wanted.

I'm sure you are more shocked then I was and that you are totally picking up on my excitement as I recite these two spectacular true events.

Now would be the best time to revisit the six simple exclusive steps that made everything happen and teach you how to effectively set them into motion, for *your* fondest desires.

The Six Simple & Straightforward Exclusive Steps for Fortunes:

1. *KNOW* that **you** *CAN* have *ANYTHING* your heart desires.
2. *Describe every detail* of your desire, out loud or on paper.
3. *Make up your mind* that you *WILL* get what you want.
4. *Fine tune your feelings* by establishing a state of certainty.
5. *Follow all actions* you are gravitated towards.
6. *Take over ownership* of your heart's desire.

Simple & Straightforward Exclusive Steps # 1:

1. *KNOW* that **you** *CAN* have *ANYTHING* your heart desires.

There is not a single thing under the sun that you can not stake your claim on if you truly desire it in your heart. There is a very vast difference between desires of the heart and desires of the head. The power within you is immense and it is not influenced by unfelt fancies. Every heart-felt desire we have is always accompanied by a gratifying feeling. The desires of our heads are just thoughts of things we think we would enjoy but evoke no emotion.

I truly desired a 1994 Dodge Shadow convertible, green with a cream-colored top. I could care less about impressing anyone. Imagining my self behind the wheel made me feel incredible.

The devastating mistake that most people make when it comes to manifesting their heart's desires is that they automatically put a price tag on their dream and fasten on to dollar digits when their full focus should be on the object of their desire. More important than only focusing on the image of our desire would be to focus on the feeling, derived from having the desire fulfilled, and what that feeling would bring to our life, overall.

The moment I definitely decided that I desired a Movado, I could have considered the hefty cost of that kind of watch but by this time, I knew the way that manifesting worked, so money never crossed my mind. If you tune into your inner wisdom, it will confirm for you that money was never meant to control us but that we were meant to control money. You can master money when you cast aside the world wide spell that money is something to be feared or worried over. Wealthy people see past this bad habit and keep their eye on the prize, not the price.

Together, the two Movado watches I wanted would have cost me close to $2K, with tax, but because I did not let money enter into the equation, I got the first one as a gift, from my sister, and I only shelled out $50.00 for the second one. The same scenario went for my dream car. I had instant access to $5,000.00 for any vehicle I wanted and it ended up only costing me $3,500.00 for the convertible. Throughout this book, we will be deliberately breaking you out of the bad habit of waking up every day with money worries in the back of your mind and replacing them with thoughts of fearless fortunes.

The only thing you need to *KNOW* for right now is that **you** *CAN* have *ANYTHING* your heart desires. We will dig up your deep-seated desires and most pressing passions, in Chapter 11. Therefore, do not decipher if your desires are from your head or your heart while we are only a fraction of the way through the book. Set aside the need to figure out what you want, for the time being. You will know exactly what to do, at the right time!

Simple & Straightforward Exclusive Steps # 2:

2. *Describe every detail* of your desire, out loud or on paper.

Writing is igniting and sends a direct signal to the power within, addressing that which you seriously want. Speaking your specific desire, out loud, is just as effective as putting it on paper, if your words are spoken from a stance of absolute certainty. *Never forget* that it is your birthright to turn inward for whatever you would like to manifest on the outside.

Your detailed desires should be summarized in a single specific sentence, like the list, below:

1. 1994 Dodge Shadow Convertible, green with a cream top.
2. Movado Watch, gold band with a black face plate.
3. Movado Watch, silver band with a white face plate.
4. 9 day Caribbean Cruise in the month of July.
5. Beige Ugg Boots in a size 7.
6. 2 Retro Giclee Lamps for living room.
7. Green and gold Dichroic glass bracelet.
8. Double my income from $45K to $90K in 60 days.
9. King Sized Brown Suede Comforter for bedroom.
10. Put $25.00 into savings, every Friday, until Christmas.

No specifications = No manifestations

It amazes me that most people never take the time to determine the definite desires that would make them the happiest person alive. No person on earth has the power to stop us from figuring out what we want and then going for it, full force. The predominant pattern of the world is to prevent disappointment by having no dreams at all. You can swiftly side step this pattern because you took the time to track down a formula that you can apply, to turn all dreams into actual reality. Knowing that you will not be let down, you will want to designate a day when you can brainstorm for a few hours and hone in on your heart's desires.

It is never enough to say that you want more money. As you already realize, this method works for no one. You need to be specific. Exactly *how much* more money, a month, do you want? Do you desire a six-figure salary a year or a six-figure annual income from home? Are you aware of what figures factor into $100K annually? Have you taken the time to crunch the numbers on a calculator and then, written them down? By saying you want six-figures a year, you need to break it down to $8,333.33 a month which works out to be approximately $1,923.50 a week for a total of 52 week in a calendar year.

There are millions of millionaires so there is no reason why someone with the strong desire to make six-figures or more can not unquestionably achieve this status as soon as they know their numbers. Even more important than exclusively knowing the numbers would be to determine the real motivation behind wanting more money. Does the financial figure you put on paper, feel right to you, or would another amount be a better fit? Work with the numbers until something inside of you completely clicks and arouses a feeling of freedom. **If you can feel it, you can real it!** You do not need to believe, at this present point, that this income is possible but at least allow your mind to begin to broaden about manifesting more money.

Every man thinks God is on his side. The rich and powerful
know he is.
~ Jean Anouilh (1910-1987) ~

<u>Simple & Straightforward Exclusive Steps # 3</u>:

3. *Make up your mind* that you *WILL* get what you want.

The single most important factor in my various manifestation stories was that I didn't waiver once or entertain other options. When I wanted a Movado watch, I didn't consider settling for a Fossil or Guess watch. I could have had 20 Guess watches for the price that the one Movado my sister gave me cost but that was not what I wanted and I didn't even have to spend a dollar to receive my true desire.

The hardest part of the whole process for both, the beginner and advanced go-getter, is being able to make up their minds. This is the most esteemed step, out of all of them, and the one I find the most stimulating, for several reasons. The proud feelings and sense of personal power that arises out of a definite decision is indescribable. Picking and sticking is the secret behind every success story you will ever see. Last but not least, the moment you can make your mind accept that you WILL get what you want will be the precise pivotal point when your inner guidance will start stepping in.

Intuition remains a mystery to most people because they never arrive at a definite decision and they almost always take advantage of the 1st opportunity that becomes available to them. Your life will be elevated to the next level and every experience you encounter will take on an entirely new meaning when you intentionally kick start your intuition. You can count on your intuition to assist you with inspirational ideas, shortly after you make up your mind that you WILL get what you want.

The only real valuable thing is intuition.
~ Albert Einstein (1879-1955) ~

<u>Simple & Straightforward Exclusive Steps # 4:</u>

4. *Fine tune your feelings* by establishing a state of certainty.

Those persons, who expect that they will have what they want, radiate an aura of certainty. Those persons who are centered in certainty do not have a worry in the world about when or how their heart's desire is going to manifest because they already feel that it is a "done deal". It is easy to enter into the state of certainty after you have put the deep thought into defining your desires and then making your mind, absolutely accept what you want. The hard work is out of the way and you can confidently detach from dwelling on your heart's desire because you've already put all the thought required for setting your manifestation into motion.

In the previous step, you made up your mind that you would get what you want. That resolution should have eliminated every excuse that could come up for depriving yourself of what you desire. If you find yourself feeling uncertain or discouraged, you still have some fine tuning to do before beginning the next step. The fastest way to fine tune your feelings is by informing your mind that you insist on having what you want and you will not take no for an answer, any longer. Stomp your foot on the floor, if you have to, and tell your mind who the real boss is in your life.

You KNOW that you have the power within you to move mountains. You are authorized to tap into this power when you have accepted your rightful responsibility, which is to rule your own mind. Regain control over opposing thoughts that used to talk you out of what you want and refuse to allow the doubts of others to enter into your self-assured mind. Now is when you will lock on, like a latch, to the object of your desire and the feelings it encompasses that ensures receipt of your prized possession.

Simple & Straightforward Exclusive Steps # 5:

5. *Follow all actions* you are gravitated towards.

This is the step where most people start to waiver or turn back, altogether. They make the mistake of dismissing ideas that seem too simple, and seek out different, more difficult ideas that diminish their motivation. No one would dare do this if they were aware that this is the part of the process where our inner power or infinite intelligence, within, rightfully takes on the responsibility of orchestrating the perfect plans for delivering our heart's desires.

All too often, I hear people plea for some sort of supernatural assistance or pray for the heavens to help them and if we did everything on our end up until this point, we have every right to start expecting such help. The problem has never been that the help isn't there but that we have a hard time releasing our need to control external events. Everyone has heard the famous saying "Let go and let God" but no one has been provided with the game plan that dictates the perfect time to back off. This is the step where we let go and allow the answers to come to us. If you catch yourself hunting down a direction or relentlessly looking for a lead, then that is a clear indication that you are ignoring the uncomplicated ideas that are coming through to your conscience, from within.

This is the step that can make or break our connection to receiving what we want, so let's take the time to solidify this step by reflecting on both of my Movado watch manifestations while correlating them to the simple six steps for effective reinforcement.

Watch # 1: Gold Band with a Black Face Plate

Step 1: Know that you can have anything your heart desires.
- I was, in no way, envious of the watches my co-workers wore, but after seeing so many sparkling wrist pieces, I sincerely started desiring one of my own.

Step 2: Describe every detail of your desire, out loud, or on paper.
- I didn't know the exact details to the Movado I wanted, at first, but I still wrote down my desire, in my notebook. That weekend, my friends and I felt drawn to the outlets, for the day. It wasn't until we were shopping at the outlets that I spotted a Movado store and I felt inspired to see their selection.

Step 3: Make up your mind that you WILL get what you want.
- After trying on several watches, I made a definite decision on which one I wanted, then I wrote down the details in my notebook.

Step 4: Fine tune your feelings by establishing a state of certainty.
- When I went to work, the following Monday, and I saw the empty Movado box in the garbage can, I didn't think it was a coincidence, but rather, I considered it as a reassuring sign that my watch was on the way. I was fortunate to get a sign but even if I hadn't, I still would have expected what I wanted, after making my specific selection, like I did with the Dodge Shadow.

Step 5: Follow all actions you are gravitated towards.
- Out of nowhere, my cousin invited me and my sister over for brunch. I was naturally inclined, in wanting to spend that Saturday with my family, so I gladly accepted.

Step 6: Take over ownership of your heart's desires.
- My sister gave me the exact watch, I wanted, as a gift.

Watch # 2: Silver Band with a White Face Plate

Step 1: Know that you can have anything your heart desires.
- I loved how classy my 1st Movado made me feel and I wanted another one to match the outfits that the gold one didn't go with.

Step 2: Describe every detail of your desire, out loud, or on paper.
- Silver band with a white face plate and the trademark signature diamond spec on the top as always.

Step 3: Make up your mind that you WILL get what you want.
  My expectancy level significantly increased in this area, after carefully analyzing all of my previous manifestations, so I instantaneously made up my mind about getting the second specific watch I wanted.

Step 4: Fine tune your feelings by establishing a state of certainty.
- After my mind was made up, that I would receive what I wanted, I automatically released all thoughts about how or when I would receive what I wanted, and I started to feel as though I was already wearing the watch on my right wrist.

Step 5: Follow all actions you are gravitated towards.
- Out of impulse, I asked my friend Melissa to stop at the up-coming 7-11 for a drink before dropping me off, home.

Step 6: Take over ownership of your heart's desires.

- The person, who had my silver Movado watch with the white face plate, was a customer at the 7-11 that we had spontaneously stopped at, and he sold me an $800.00 for $50.00.

Simple & Straightforward Exclusive Steps # 6:

6. *Take over ownership* of your heart's desires.

There is no greater feeling in the world, than the one you will experience, when you have in your possession, the very thing that you desire. You will most certainly take over ownership of your heart's desire, no matter what it may be, if you dutifully followed the first five steps of this formula. Your heart's desire will come to you, in wondrous ways, after you take any traditional type actions that you feel inspired to, from within.

The power inside of you is not only immense but it is also all-knowing and it has access to an unlimited amount of resources for ingeniously delivering your heart's desire. You will never need to worry about how or when your desire is going to arrive as long as you maintain the appropriate attitude and take any action that is within your power to perform. The moment your mind is made up that you will get what you want, any actions that you are expected to take will rapidly race through your mind, causing you to feel massively motivated.

There will also be times where you have made up your mind that you will get what you want and not a single action will arrive at that moment. The power, within, will always tell you when to make a move and your only concern should be in maintaining your certainty, at all times, if no inspired actions are arising. If you force yourself to take action, when you are not being guided to do so, you could interfere with the flow and accidentally end up in a different location than *where* and/or *when* your desire was initially going to be delivered.

In other words, if you insist on doing things your way, then expect for your life to stay the same as it has always been. If on the other hand, you want to start continuously creating enchanting experiences and enjoying everything you could ever desire, then it is time to trust the wisdom within, over the world's way. The way of the world is to break you back, having you work harder while you're searching everywhere else but within, for wealth. The wisdom, within, told you, along time ago, how to get your hands on the all wealth you want but your mind most likely contested that either this was too good to be true or that is was much too easy to possibly work.

There is no way to say what route the power, within, will walk us on, to receive our hearts desire, but what I can confirm from repeated experience is that when you truly trust yourself, you will always act on the inner prompting that will directly lead you to your desire each and every time.

When I wanted to take over ownership of my Dodge Shadow convertible, the action steps were drastically different from what I was inspired to do, in taking over ownership of both my Movado watches. Either way, I always KNEW what I needed to do and acted accordingly.

The first thing I was inspired to do, when I wanted my custom convertible, was to collect all the auto mart magazines I could get my hands on. The next step was to start making my "2-question" phone calls. I would ask the sales man if they had a 1994 Dodge Shadow convertible, green with a cream-colored top and when they said, "No", I would ask them if they knew where I could get it. I didn't mind making all those calls, because it was a breeze, and for every "No" I got, I felt that much closer to getting what I wanted. My excitement increased, with every inspired step I took.

After I called every dealership in my state, the idea to ask my father, down in Florida, to call around there, immediately came to mind. I quickly called my Dad, who was happy to help, and then I thought to call the 2 closest surrounding states, while waiting to hear back from him. When neither of us found what we were looking for, the opportunity to take a look at the Cavalier came into play. I went along for the ride and took a look at the Cavalier. That same night, I had a strong craving for pizza and I went with my gut reaction. My intuition insisted I leave my number on some stranger's car and I did. For 5 straight days, I couldn't think of any other actions to take so, I stayed centered, in my certainty. That Friday, I got a phone call from the stranger who I intuitively left my number for and she led me to my dream car. I took over ownership in 2 weeks.

As far as my **gold** Movado watch, the only thing I felt inspired to do was to write my desire down in my notebook. That weekend, I found myself face-to-face with a Movado store and I felt compelled to try on a few watches so I could decide on the one I wanted. I made my definite decision and wrote down the details in my notebook. I saw it as a sign that I would be getting my Movado, when I came across the empty box that week, while I was at work. During the week, my cousin had called and invited me over for Saturday. I looked forward to seeing my family very much and that day, my sister gave me the exact watch I wanted, as an unexpected gift. I didn't really do anything other than write down that I wanted a Movado watch and then I faithfully tried on a few, to make my ultimate choice.

I put in even less effort to get my **silver** Movado, the following week. The only thing I felt inspired to do was to write down the new specifications in my notebook. I do remember imagining the watch as already being on my right wrist and that was enough to make me maintain my certainty that I would get it. That weekend, I spent the day having fun with my friend and spontaneously asked her to stop at the store for a drink. The man, who had my watch, was waiting at that location for someone to buy exactly what I wanted and I was elated to give him $50.00 for the exceedingly expensive watch I insisted on owning.

We will wrap up this chapter by emphasizing on the most profitable points that will serve you, in the immediate moment, and sustain you through all future ambitions.

Let everyone sweep in front of his own door, and the whole world will be clean.
~ Johann Wolfgang von Goethe (1749-1832) ~

Profitable Point 1: No longer concern yourself with the economy and latest headline news. Commit to correcting your own finances. The economy is averaged out, according the accumulation of each individual's debt to income ratio and the only way that the economy will improve is when each individual concentrates on rectifying his/her own financial status. Clean up your own bank account and the whole world can then be wealthy.

Profitable Point 2: Be bold and transcend the way that 97% of the people in this world think about money by bustling through your own bordered beliefs.

Profitable Point 3: For your own soul's sake, stop listening to the doubts of others and take leadership over your life, by mastering your own mind.

Profitable Point 4: Let your first definitive decision be that you will transition from the world's way of working harder and start tuning into the wisdom, within, for guaranteed guidance. There is much to be gained, from the old cliché, that the wealthy people of this world follow which is, "Work smarter, not harder".

Profitable Point 5: Before falling off to sleep tonight, give yourself permission to picture, for a minimum of 5 minutes how much happier your life will be when you fearlessly follow the formula and allow yourself to manifest your unique set of desires.

The Forgotten Realm Where Riches Rule

The positive thinker sees the invisible, feels the intangible and achieves the impossible.
~ Anonymous ~

You can enter the forgotten realm where riches rule as soon as you are freed from all feelings of want and need. Desire without attachment is always welcome within this wonderful realm but desperation has no right to trespass in such a prosperous place. Want and need are denied, at the door, because they contradict everything that this realm represents.

Did the previous paragraph anger you at all and bring to mind all the bills you have coming up this month? Be relieved if that was your initial reaction, because this chapter contains the insight for transforming feelings of want and need into detached desiring that is able to achieve the impossible. You will gain all the knowledge you need to flip switch your feeling, from desperation to manifestation.

Those that live in a constant state of wanting and needing can be categorized as the "barely getting by" group. Those that live in a constant state of optimism and high hopes can be categorized as the "above average" group. And then, there are those that live in a constant state of certainty and expectation, who can be categorized as the "elite earners" of our world.

Our feelings and frame of mind most certainly determine our degree of wealth. I have yet to come across a school or institution that teaches us humans how to harness our feelings and intentionally direct our own minds, like a captain does his crew to the desired destination. Mind power, without passion, is like being aboard a luxurious cruise ship, without an engine. When you can master the skill of mustering up specific certain feelings then you can powerfully pull in all of those things that once seemed out of your reach.

The reason why this realm is classified as "forgotten" is because human behavior has people fearing their feelings and resorting to relentless thinking or great physical exertion, with mediocre results. Your feelings are your only form of communication with the power that worketh in you and the same unseen force that is orchestrating everything in the invisible realm throughout the entire Universe. This fact will clear up any confusion as to why our sincerest prayers, of the past, went unanswered.

If you were to plant several strawberry seeds, would you not be surprised if apricots started to sprout? Why is it then that when we pray our problems, we expect solutions to surface? We have all heard that you reap what you sow. It would make sense then to start **speaking the solution rather then praying the problem.** You can speed up the solution to any dire circumstance when you can find the feeling, from within, that the solution has already arrived.

For 10 years, I desired to transform my figure from a size 16 to a size 6. I maintained my size 16 because I kept repeating that size to myself whereas I should have been affirming my desirable size 6. I went with the world's way to lose weight which was diet and exercise but my size barely budged. Can you figure out what my frame of mind was for all these years and the persistent feelings I was walking around with? My frame of mind was on weight loss and my steadfast feelings were centered in dread, for the actions I would need to take to lose weight.

On the next page I am going to share with you how I was able to drop 4 pant sizes per month and maintain a size 6 for the past 2 years when I discovered how to flip switch my feelings instantly!!!

When I finally reached the point where I was sick of "wanting" to lose weight and "needing" to stick to some sort of deprivation diet, I dug down deep, within myself, to get to the bottom of why I desired to be a size 6 for so long. It dawned on me, in that instant, that my main motivation for desiring to be a size 6 was to feel great from the inside, out. Finally...I found the feeling and my focus detracted from losing weight to feeling great!!!

That day I made the definite decision that I would dedicate my frame of mind to feeling great and abandon all thoughts about losing weight. My frame of mind also shifted from being a size 16 to seeing myself as a size 6. Focusing on feeling great made me feel great, instantaneously, whereas focusing on losing weight always made me feel awful. Out of that definite decision, came the inspiration that I can eat anything I want as long as it makes me feel great and to find a physical activity that I would desire to do, 4 days a week, because it feels great while I am doing it. I stopped counting calories and following work out programs that promised weight loss but I dreaded doing. My motivation was at an all time high, from that day forward, and I found an assortment of activities that I absolutely loved doing. I became addicted to feeling great and slipped into a size 6, three times faster than I would have had I went with any conventional weight loss plan.

We have to put an end to placing our attention on the wrong focal points and forcing ourselves to do things that we dread. We will soon be able to start manifesting every good fortune that we desire once we swap out "wanting and needing" for "believing and receiving". Your feelings are powerful forces that either repel what you want, in the worst way, or pull in, like a magnet, those things that you desire with detachment. Never fear your feelings because you have the power to master them this very day and make them start serving you like they were always intended to.

If you doubt that your feelings are the fertile forces that create your current reality and are responsible for the experiences you encounter, then you will want to keep an open mind to this truth for when you are really ready to turn all your dreams of opulence into concrete conditions. Spend the next 2 minutes, soaking up the scripture below, and then we will magnify its meaning about manifesting what we desire in our world.

> Now faith is the substance of things hoped for, the evidence of things not seen.
> ~ Hebrews 11:1 (KJV) ~

The perceptive person, who takes the time to assimilate the scripture above and actually applies it to every area of their life, will have earned the right to receive everything that they desire.

The word, "faith" is thrown around so loosely these days, having lost its original definition along the way. Faith is not to be mistaken for finger-crossing nervousness or wishing for the best but settling for scraps that come your way. The Dictionary.com definition for *faith* is "confidence or trust in a person or thing". True trust is the antidote for destroying all doubt. Therefore, faith is complete confidence and total trust. Most people treat faith like a leaf, blowing around in the wind. They release their faith, worrying that it will end up eventually evaporating into thin air or land them in a place that they didn't pick. Some synonyms for faith are *acceptance, assurance, certainty and conviction.*

You will be delighted when you discover what "substance" represents to us in the context of this scripture. The Dictionary.com definition for *substance* is "that of which a thing consists; physical matter or material". We are being exposed to the **failproof instructions** for converting invisible ideas into physical matter.

It is obvious that "things hoped for" are those things that we desire with our whole heart. The last line gives me chills and goose bumps because it provides us with the firm confirmation that we will have what we desire!!! The Dictionary.com definition for *evidence* is "to make evident or clear; show clearly; manifest". Some synonyms for evidence are *authentication, demonstration, validation and verification*.

Now that we are finished exploring the factual definitions for the words, within the scripture we are contemplating, let's formulate 3 rephrased versions for the purpose of fueling your fire!

King James Version of Hebrews 11:1:
Now faith is the substance of things hoped for, the evidence of things not seen.

Rephrased Version # 1:
Now *certainty* is the physical matter that molds our heart's desire, the confirmation that we will see what was initially an invisible idea in our mind.

Rephrased Version # 2:
Now *conviction* is the physical fabric that adds form to our dearest dreams, the validation that we will see what was initially an invisible idea in our mind.

Rephrased Version # 3:
Now *assurance* is the physical material that objectifies our highest hopes, the verification that we will see what was initially an invisible idea in our mind.

The forgotten realm where riches rule is where the creator of this majestic world resides and everyone is encouraged to enter this realm as the co-creator we were all born to be. Your lack of awareness about this realm and your reservations about this realm are what cause you to remain an outsider. The doors will open wide for the guest that greets the guard, with resounding certainty of their right to enter, and an outline of the detailed desires they will be requesting while inside this realm. If you can imagine it in your mind's eye, you can call it forth, here. Nothing is impossible, inside this sacred space.

Think about the thousand of different kinds and colored fish that fill our oceans. Consider the fascinating flavors, form and collection of colors, our fruit fields yield. Take into account, the tiger's fierce striping and the leopard's near perfect pattern. Bring to mind, the various landscape scenes you have witness with your own eyes, and then try to tell me that outrageous creativity is in any way impossible or only limited by our own minds. The same invisible force, that fathomed and gave form to these intricate ideas, is embedded in your very being. It is that persistent push, within, that insists you enjoy creating everything that you desire.

Do not delay another day by questioning your ability and authority to fill your intimate surroundings with all the things that give you great joy. You will have found your true faith when you genuinely expect for experiences to revolve around your most gratifying emotions. The burden we bear when we erroneously try to alter the true nature of our being is that we rob ourselves of the right to freely co-create.

We are born as Human Beings who do everything imaginable to become "Human Head Strong" and "Human Hard Workers". Has your compulsive thinking or physical efforts allotted you the lifestyle you envision? Thoughts are worth a dime a dozen and even the most physically fit endure exhaustion but the human, who is centered in certainty, knows how to manifest…smoothly.

Can you honestly say that most people you meet, express certainty, or send off vibes of insecurity? Insecurity is a powerful feeling that vibrates in the very being of the majority you meet. Insecurity discharges a strong energy that expels every good fortune that these innocent individuals are entitled to and it can consciously be converted into certainty, the moment they become mindful of what is occurring. Certainty sends out strong signals of enticing expectant energy and attracts the attention of all great fortune.

Right now, let's recapture the revelation revealed in Hebrews 11:1, and in the next chapter, I will share with you *how* this powerful principle freed me from $20K debt in 3 days.

Rephrased Version # 1:
Now *certainty* is the physical matter that molds our heart's desire, the confirmation that we will see what was initially an invisible idea in our mind.

Everything you could hope to get your hands on is made up of matter, supplied by nature such as metal, mineral, plastic, wood, wool, etc. Exotic sports cars are made from metal, diamonds are made from minerals, computers are comprised of plastic, dream homes are made with wood, paper money is made from trees and fashionable clothes are created from wool. An encyclopedia would not be extensive enough to include the trillions of items that are manufactured from natural matter.

The question then is, "Where does this natural matter originate from"? Just like electricity, all natural matter emerges from an unseen source. An invisible, intelligent source supplied us with all of these rich resources and **provided us with the procedure** for molding our imaginary ideas into corporeal matter.

Life is like a grand buffet. Everything we could ever enjoy is right in front of our faces and readily available but we have to build up the courage to take what we want. The certainty that is required to acquire all that you desire can not be brought, by means of money. If you expect to establish certainty, you will need to transfer all the trust you have placed in manufactured money and put all that trust back into true power that thrives in the center of your being.

Inside of you is the only authentic money maker and magnet that patiently waits for you to turn within, for phenomenal prospering power. By placing all your faith in printed money, you are mistakenly severing yourself from the source of all your wealth. It may be the most mentally difficult thing, you will have to do, but despite seeing everyone, you are surrounded by, professing their undying faith in the dollar bill, the only opportunity you have, to exceedingly surpass everyone, who are struggling financially, is by believing in yourself for a c-h-a-n-g-e.

You can call forth more money than you know what to do with when your attitude about abundance is anchored in the power within, instead of falsely fixating on physical objects that subconsciously become obstacles, in the mind that is misplacing their power. Your certainty, in yourself, is the power that will produce the substance of *any specific thing* you desire, containing confirmation that you have correctly secured that particular thing, with your faith. Your sustained certainty is needed to strengthen the substance process and speed up the delivery date.

When you are advised, in advance, of a realistic travel time, it is much more likely that you will sustain your certainty. Those, who are unable to manifest, do not understand the non-negotiable ingredient of certainty and they allow doubt to dominate, after a day or two. I have found, from dissecting every desire I intentionally set out to manifest, that it takes me anywhere from the same day to a few days or up to two weeks, typically, to take over ownership. Anything that takes over two weeks is a clear indication to me that I must remove any last little lingering doubt, by restoring my certainty.

You can restore your certainty by making up your mind up that you do not need permission or approval from anyone, to receive anything that you desire. God does not deny anyone, of the things that they desire, regardless of what religious enthusiasts sometimes say, as their way of justifying their own fragile faith. Your doubt will deny you of your desire, every time, if you fail to assert your certainty. The heavens are happiest when they witness human beings, who use the power of their will, to trust their own opinions, over those of others and who confidently co-create, by controlling the thoughts that enter their mind.

Your work is never to convince another person to believe on your behalf or free them from their doubt. Your work will always be in banishing all of your doubt, to the best of your ability, that has built up throughout the years and accept your freedom to design the life you love, by filling that space with *certainty* in its place. Once you get a tiny taste of how quickly *certainty* can accommodate your appetite for good fortune, you will wonder why you digested *doubt* for all those years.

We will wrap up this chapter, by crystallizing the most profitable points about *certainty* that will serve you in the immediate moment and sustain you through all future ambitions.

Profitable Point 1: *Certainty* is "desiring without requiring". You can manifest anything that you desire but do not need. "Want and need" send out strong signals of doubt that disenables the power to pull in your desire. *Certainty* sends out strong signals that you are past the point of desiring and rooted in having already received your desire, which invariably produces the power to promptly pull in your desire, with precision.

Profitable Point 2: *Certainty* knows that it will absolutely take over ownership of its definite desire and has no need to track time because it is always on alert, in the present moment, for promptings or attention-tugging actions to take.

Profitable Point 3: *Certainty* does not resist the doubts of others because there is no need to defend something when you know, deep down, what the outcome will be. If any doubt is coming from your close friends or family members, you can be confident that they will come around, at the right time, and start asking for your advice, after you get yourself situated.

Profitable Point 4: Those individuals, who courageously step into *certainty*, when surrounded by skeptics, will be richly rewarded. Subsequently, they will find themselves placed in leadership positions, teaching the people they love, on how to transform their own lives, faster than they ever thought possible!

Completely Freed from Debt in 3 Days

Jesus said to him, If you can believe; all things are possible to him that believes.
~ Mark 9:23 (A.K.J.V.) ~

By the time I was twenty years old, I had a collection of 15 charge cards. On my flight back from Florida one year, Southwest was giving away prizes to the first person, who waived in the air, whatever item it was that they called out. The airline auctioned off a case of peanuts to the traveler with the most credit cards. Guess who the winner was of the credit card contest? The runner up only had 11 charge cards and I beat him by 4, making me the proud new owner of 100 packets of peanuts.

My compulsive spending and car loan dug me $20K in debt. For four years, I woke up every day, feeling weighed down by my debt. I searched diligently for a way to wipe out my mountainous balance. I wanted nothing to do with consolidation programs because I was not willing to wait 5 more years for debt freedom. Defaulting on my debt was never an option in my mind because my credit score means too much to me and I would rather pay my monthly minimums for the rest of my life then back out of my obligations. I looked into money making opportunities and every debt relief option being offered but none of them moved me. In the back of my mind, I just knew there had to be a way to bang out my balance and start establishing a substantial savings.

My belief that "nothing is impossible and that ALL things ARE possible" is the attitude that entitled me to be freed from debt in 3 days. There is no reason why you must remain burdened by debt, another day. You can radically reverse your financial situation when you make the drastic discernment, like I did when I was twenty four years old. We are about to discover what most of the multitude is doing wrong in regards to dealing with debt and I will reveal the fastest approach to financial freedom.

When I think back to that day, 6 years ago, when I instantly wiped out my debt, I still wonder sometimes, why I was one of the fortunate few who, by chance, provoked the power of a paradigm shift while millions of others sought the same solution but still struggle to this day with money matters. I realize now that the reason why I was the recipient of such revolutionary information is because I not only took immediate action, when internally instructed to do so, but it was my life's calling to communicate these principles to the world and I would not allow anything to deter me from my destiny.

I initially came across the term "paradigm shift" in the best selling book, "The 7 Habits of Highly Effective People", by Stephen R. Covey. The Dictionary.com definition for *paradigm shift* is "a fundamental change in approach or assumptions". From firsthand experience, I like to explain a paradigm shift as replacing a habitual thought structure on the spur of the moment, resulting in a more suitable thought structure for rapid results.

I don't know where the determination came from, out of no where, but one day after being distressed over my debt for 4 consecutive years, I officially reached my breaking point. I remember, like it was yesterday, I was standing in my hallway and in the midst of catching myself starting to sink into depressing thoughts about all the money I owed, I suddenly snapped back and dauntlessly declared out load, "I AM DONE WITH DEBT".

These 5 seemingly insignificant words forever changed my finances and disclosed to me the potent missing piece that most people will never know about but, you will, before the end of this chapter.

I did not discuss my declaration about being done with debt, to anyone, because the affirmation I made in my hallway had completely cast out all thoughts about debt from my mind.

That definitive day, when I announced to myself that I was done with debt, I meant it!!! Have you ever cared about something for so long that you got sick and tired about constantly hoping for it happen so you one day decide that it isn't even worth it? That day, in my hallway, I turned my back on debt and I could honestly care less how it was all going to play out because in my mind, I was done.

On the 3rd day, after emphatically abandoning my debt, my boyfriend sat me down, to share an idea that he had been bouncing back and forth in his head. He confided in me that he despised my debt as much as I did because his parents raised him to pay for everything he wanted, with crisp cash and he couldn't relate to my credit card problem because he was taught how to master money as an adolescent. He informed me that after thoroughly thinking things over, he had desired and definitely decided to pull out of his equity, the entire amount needed to satisfy all of my accumulated debts. He did all his homework, before sitting me down and presenting me with the perfect plan for transforming my debt into a steady stream of financial security.

My boyfriend's monthly mortgage would be increased by $100.00 if we went through with the refinance. My monthly minimums were averaging me approximately $800.00 at the time. We agreed that I would give him the additional $100.00 every month and deposit the remaining $700.00 into a savings account. I couldn't resist the temptation to ask my boyfriend how long he had been thinking about this brilliant idea of his and I was affectionately amused when he responded that he conceived this idea only 3 days ago, which was the very same day I attested, in my hallway, "I AM DONE WITH DEBT". Within 3 weeks, we were in possession of the certified check from the bank, and I paid off every outstanding debt that was in my name. I have long since paid my boyfriend back the full amount he financed for me and to this day, I am grateful to him for taking such a big risk with his money, on my behalf.

A majority of manifestation authors do not like to dispense the details to how their desires unfold, for one of two reasons. First, they do not want the reader to assume that things will work out the same way, for their specific situation, because everyone's experience will be unique so, do not make the mistake of fixating on anyone else's sequence, for your own expected outcome. Once we get you into the flow of making precise definite decisions, you will naturally release your need to know how everything will happen. The other reason why most manifestation authors do not dispense the details about how designated desires unfold is because their passion lies in distributing other people's manifestation stories and they can not correctly explain every key component because they never personally experienced the process.

The potent missing piece that eludes the minds of most people is the permeating power within the words "I AM". Like a broken record, I repeated to myself every day for 4 years that "I AM in debt"…"I AM in debt"…"I AM in debt". My debt did not go away until the day I turned it all around by proclaiming "I AM done with debt".

We have all developed the debilitating mindset that dismisses the present point of power by making statements that start with "I wish" or "I will be" instead of saying, "I AM", when it comes to all the things that would make us happy. Almost everyone I ask will admit that they do this, confessing that they feel like they are lying to themselves when they say, "I AM", about anything that doesn't line up with their current conditions. Your present reality is a perfect match that mirrors all the mental and audible *I AM* affirmations you made, prior to this moment.

Every passing minute is another chance to turn it all around.
~ The Movie Vanilla Sky ~

You have the opportunity to turn your finances and any-thing else, around this passing minute, but you must accept that "I wish" and "I will be" are like seeds that produce weeds, sabotaging your progress. *I wish* and *I will be* are the same as saying "I AM NOT". I wish I was rich because I am not. I will be wealthy one day because right now I am not.

The power within you operates from the highest order of in-telligence and it can not create anything that affirms "I AM NOT" but *it will give life* to all that affirms "I AM". You can alter any area of your life when you acknowledge the wisdom of adapting the "I AM" mindset to anything you would like to come to life.

And God said unto Moses, I AM THAT I AM: and he said, Thus shalt thou say unto the children of Israel, I AM hath sent me unto you.
~ Exodus 3:14 (K.J.V.) ~

The cause of all creation can be called *I AM*, as indicated above, because it encompasses everything that exists and it takes credit for anything that is alive or observable. Human beings are the only offspring, consecrated with the capability to consciously create their every experience and environment on earth. The power to reposition our lot in life is dependent on the value we put into the transforming forces that cater to the command following, "I AM".

As we learnt in the last chapter, certainty is the substance of things hoped for and more often than not, most people surrender their only ticket, to bountiful abundance, by entertaining the belief that "it must not be God's will for me to (fill in the blank)".

If someone is quick to come to this conclusion then that means this particular individual did not know how to play their part in the manifestation process or it was not truly within their will if they were that laid back about pardoning their preference.

In my favorite book, "Your Faith Is Your Fortune", by Neville Goddard, the true meaning of what God's will and not what my will really represents was distinguished in the same way that it was made known to me, the day I rid myself of debt. The wisdom of God's will, over our will, is that God's will always asserts, "IT **IS** DONE" and our will always affirms, "IT IS **NOT** DONE".

Anything you attempt to do that could increase your income or eliminate existing expenses will back fire if your mindset does not differ from the one that created the present problem and keeps them in place. You can not realistically expect to call forth fortunes if you continue to maintain the "I AM NOT RICH" mantra and mentality. Let those that do not know any better, stay set in their ways if they *will*, while reinforcing all that they are **not**, but at least allow yourself to consider everything you can create, after absorbing the *I AM* approach.

Since the thoughts you think and the beliefs you have are determined by you alone, it is your task to tell them the way things will be, when you are ready to apply the formula, in full. In chapter 15, Strive for Five and Ignite Your Drive, we will begin working with the, *I AM* approach, for accelerated advancement, in any direction you desire. For the time being, whenever your mind attempts to remind you of your current incomplete reality, you will no longer tolerate these thoughts that have caused it to be incomplete by powerfully affirming "I AM" (blank) but got good at pushing it away by believing the opposite.

If you desire to be rich, then the wisdom within is saying, "I AM already rich", wishing to express that on the outside. Others think that they are lying to themselves when they make *I AM* affirmations, based on outward observations, but because they do not know or believe that the invisible inner realm is the cause, of all outside objects that appear, they deny every desire. Therefore, look at it like *denying rather then lying* if you feel yourself falling into that trap.

All things are possible to him that believes but beliefs must be rightfully rooted inward if an outward manifestation is anticipated. "All things are possible" embraces every outcome you could concoct and dream up, without any cap on your creativity. If you are willing to break free, from the beliefs that bind you, you will rush into the reality where all things are readily possible.

I originated and held onto the belief that there had to be a way to pay off $20K, all at once and once and for all. The same option to refinance existed when I first fashioned the idea of being out of debt but I blocked it, for all those years, by continuing to believe I was in debt instead of insisting, "I AM DONE WITH DEBT". I knew the possibility to pay off that lump sum could somehow come about but every day, I silently said, deep down, "I AM IN DEBT". My desire didn't see the light of day because the power, within my being, only answers to *I AM*. I AM to blame for all those years that I was in debt and I AM responsible for releasing it out of my reality.

True believing takes place in the center of your being. If you rely on your mind power alone, your manifestations could take months or even years. The trick to powerfully pulling in your desires is by faithfully following the 3 steps below:

1. Make a definite decision, based on what you truly desire. Remember, ALL things ARE possible to him/her that believes so do not seek out other people's opinions.

2. Begin believing that your definite decision is a done deal, by thinking only thoughts that support "IT IS DONE".

3. Most important, make it impossible for your desire, not to manifest, by centering yourself in the firm feeling of *I AM*, right this instant, in receipt of that very thing.

You will physically feel your power, from within, activating and awakening when all 3 steps are applied in the order they are listed. When you mentally prepare yourself in advance, to persevere, up until the finish line, you drastically shorten the distance between merging with your manifestation. Once you get your feet wet, with these steps, you will become unstoppable and all the times that you deprived yourself of what you wanted, we will but a vague and distant memory.

Shaking Off the Shackles of Other People's Opinions

Then touched he their eyes, saying, According to your faith be it
done unto you.
~ Matthew 9:29 (A.S.V.) ~

We live in a faithless world, filled with people who possess
the power to make miracles manifest, but they find it impossible to
believe in the best because they are persuaded to pay attention to all
of the bad things. You do realize that you have the right and
responsibility to decide, this fine day, whether you will play for the
winning team that believes in the best or play for the losing team
that focuses on failure? No one will hold it against you for having
the guts to go for greatness and imagine how many people you will
inspire by daring to be different.

There is no escaping the law of cause and effect that acts accordingly, every time anyone initiates an idea. Your faith is the
cause of every experience that you will bring into being. Your faith
is like a standard seed, planted in soil, but ten times more powerful
because when your *will* is strong, your desire can manifest the same
day. It is believed, by the majority, that most of their thoughts
make no difference in their lives, but little do they know that the
intelligence, within, imprints everything that each individual imag-
ines. The power, within, considers you too important to ignore and
it is not too much to ask that you start taking yourself as seriously.

You are endlessly encouraged to have faith in all of your
dreams and according to YOUR faith be it DONE unto YOU. It
makes no difference if your next door neighbor, best friend or
spouse does not have faith in your dreams or doubts, every step of
the way, because only YOUR faith can cause YOUR dreams to be
done unto you. There is a remarkable woman, Helene Hadsell, who
won every single contest she ever entered over the past 50 years by

holding true to her faith in the midst of millions that decided to doubt their dreams and desires.

Brace yourself because I am about to share with you the day the doctor sent my dad home from his scheduled surgery and announced that his cancer had completely disappeared, to prove to you, the unyielding power of faith.

One afternoon, approximately 4 years ago, I was on the phone with my father and as we were about to hang up, he hesitantly said that there was something else he wanted to tell me. He never wants to worry his children with anything but he knew that I would be more upset if he kept important information from me. My oldest sister, Jennifer, was a medical student at the time and she noticed an abnormal growth in my father's ear. My sister was well on her way to becoming a doctor and she said, straight out, that she was sure it was cancerous. My father then admitted that the growth had been there for a while and that it kept growing bigger but he thought that if he ignored it, eventually it would go away.

My father's friend had the same growth, in the same spot, and he had to have half of his ear clipped then surgically reconstructed. After having his knowledgeable friend inspect his ear, his buddy highly recommended the specialist that performed his procedure, handing my father the phone number to make an appointment. My father knew that my sister and his friend were most likely correct in concluding that his growth was cancerous but he wanted at least one more professional opinion.

The morning of the afternoon that my father first phoned me was the day he had the appointment with the specialist. He went on to say that the specialist confirmed that it was cancerous and that if my father did not make an immediate appointment within the next two weeks, it could spread so rapidly, beyond surgically saving. I could hear the fear in my father's voice but he was equally relieved for having caught it in time. My father and I are as close as can be but rather then go into instant panic mode, a feeling of certainty welled up, within me, while we were still speaking, that he would somehow not have to get the surgery.

As soon as I hung up with my father, I said out load "Thank you that his ear is clear; there's nothing there; whatever once was there now returns to the nothingness from which it came". These words came out of me instinctively without having to consciously formulate my confession. "Thank you that his ear is clear" is praying the specific solution instead of the problem. "There's nothing there" is faith that I already received my request. "Whatever once was there" is acknowledging the reality that something did surface. "Now returns to the nothingness from which it came" recognizes that there was a time when this growth did not exist and we do not welcome it, so it can go back to being nothing.

Immediately after making my private announcement, I knew, deep down, it was a "done deal" as I went about my day. I felt no need to say the same statement, every night before bed, because I believed it had already happened. The next week my father called me again and reminded me that his surgery was the following week. After we hung up, that was when I felt inspired to say my statement out loud, for the second time, and I released it again with full faith.

The night before my father's scheduled surgery, he called to hear my voice, saying that he would probably be in too much pain to phone me the following day but he would make sure my mom updated me, when they got home. That final phone call, with my father, still did not make me doubt that my proclamation would be fulfilled and for the last time I spoke my statement, out loud, with utmost certainty.

Early the next morning, I got a phone call, from my parent's number, and I naturally assumed that it was my mom, calling with the update. I was overjoyed, when I heard it was my father, on the other end, because he didn't sound like he was in any pain. I wasn't expecting to hear from them until late afternoon so I asked him how he was able to be home, already?

My father sounded so happy when he said that the doctor sent him home, shortly after arriving for his appointment. I automatically asked if his surgery got rescheduled for some reason and my father responded that the doctor had completely cancelled his appointment. As stunned as we both were, he went on to say that the specialist wanted to see how much the growth had spread since the last time he was there, making my dad a little nervous when the doctor said, in a rather startling tone, that he could not believe what he was seeing.

The doctor looked directly at my father and said, with such surprise, that the cancerous growth was gone. In disbelief, the doctor checked my father's ear, for the 3rd time, before definitely determining that the ailment had disappeared and that there was no way he would operate on a healthy ear. The doctor advised my father to have his ear checked, 2 more times, over the next twelve months and we are happy to report that, 4 years later, his ear is still completely clear.

This book may not be about health but the primary message in every manifestation story, that I have shared so far, is that ALL things ARE possible, according to YOUR faith. There is nothing you can not call forth for yourself and your loved ones when you are aware that faith is the cord that plugs you into the power, within. I know nothing about the health care industry and I couldn't heal my father with my bare hands but because I have working knowledge of the faith factor, what we desired was done unto us.

Best Selling Author, Louise L. Hay, shares how she healed herself of cancer in "The Power of Your Spoken Word", without any medical assistance and with the pure power of her will. You can come across an abundance of other stories, along these lines, if you have your heart set and mind made up about miraculous alternatives. However, most people have their minds made up that it is impossible to achieve your dreams and desires, via one's own personal will power, and according to each individual's faith, it is done unto them. Is it starting to register that what we choose to believe is what will "make or break" us and not some outside force?

Truth be told, faith is not resigned to religion and actually requires you to believe in yourself as opposed to something separate from yourself, if it is to work wonders. The only reason why people do not tap into their internal personal power is because some other person planted the seed in their head that it would be a sin to do such a thing. The people who plant such demoralizing seeds in the minds of others does not necessarily imply that they are intentionally trying to hinder their fellow human being, but that they are deeply invested into that belief, themselves. The people who believe that it is some sort of sin to tap into the power, within, for bringing their desires for health or wealth to pass, will spend their whole life, laboring day and night to make ends meet.

Almost all of the beliefs and thoughts that are stored in our subconscious mind were bestowed to us by other people, either in person, through books or from our beloved bible. Since the main subject matter of this book is money and, you wouldn't be reading this right now if you didn't desire more, I am going to ask that you set aside 5 minutes to really think through the following question:

What do YOU honestly believe about money, in general?

Did, "Money is the root of all evil", come to mind?

Do you desire to be rich but believe that you never will be?

Do you catch yourself worrying when money crosses your mind?

Do you often think that making more money is the most difficult thing to do?

Do you imagine having to do things you dislike, to make the money you desire?

Do you think that it is a sin to be a Multi-Millionaire when there are poor people across the globe?

Did you originate these beliefs about money or did you develop them, over the years, by observing other people who are predominantly perplexed by all matters that involve money?

Our minds are like sponges that soak up everything our eyes are drawn to, until we mature our minds, as we adults are all destined to do and we begin thinking authentic thoughts that summon the wealth of this world. You must make the conscious choice to purify your mind, by banishing all antagonistic beliefs about making more money, and allow boundless beliefs for beckoning more money, to monopolize your mind.

Now, I want you to answer the same question but with an alteration to it. For the next 5 minutes, I would like you to release ALL thoughts about what the bible says about money, as well as what other people's opinion about money are, then we can continue:

What do <u>YOU</u> honestly believe about money, in general?

If you genuinely freed your mind from other people's opinions about money and the negative notations in the bible about money then you should be blown away, by how different your answers were, the second time around. Another important piece of information you should be aware of, at this stage, is that for every negative notation about money, in the bible, there is a neutralizing notation about accumulating wealth, within the same doctrine.

Pessimistic people are inclined to recite the negative notations to support their poor attitudes while positive people are apt to recite the scriptures, regarding abundance, to support their prosperous attitudes. Neither personal preference is nobler then the other and according to each person's particular faith, it will be done unto them. We have been given the free will to fill our hearts and heads with any life building belief system we desire, so select wisely because, according to YOUR faith, be it done unto YOU.

Are you willing to trade out other people's opinions that imprison you from tapping into your personal power, in exchange for a permanent passport that permits you to explore every destination you desire? Pat yourself on the back if you answered yes because that single quality decision places you on the fast track to fortunes, as you will certainly come to see soon.

We ended the last chapter, by listing the 3 steps for powerfully pulling in your desires. You are now ready to pack a punch and blast through any barrier that might block your manifestation, by fortifying the third step. Really read through the 3 steps again, from start to finish, and resist the temptation to rush right through them, if you are genuinely devoted to making your desires manifest:

1. Make a definite decision, based on what you truly desire. Remember, ALL things ARE possible to him that believes, so do not seek out other people's opinions.

2. Begin believing that your definite decision is a done deal by thinking only thoughts that support "IT IS DONE".

3. Most importantly, make it impossible for your desire, not to manifest, by centering yourself in the firm feeling of I AM, right this instant, in receipt of that very thing.

The scripture below is another way of wording the third step:

And all things, whatsoever ye shall ask in prayer, believing, ye shall receive.
~ Matthew 21:22 (K.J.V.) ~

When I was little, I was taught that praying is praising and pleading, to an outside entity to mainly prevent evil events from happening. I was also warned against praying for sincere wishes and encouraged to commit to memory, pre-written prayers, without any guidance on custom creating my own. The following week, I would be sitting in on a new service that suggested that the kingdom of heaven was found, within each of us, and that we could/should ask for whatsoever we wanted while praying??? These complete contradictions, from when I was a child, caused me years of confusion, later on in life. In chapter 9, we will uncover, the rarely contemplated cause, of these conflicting contradictions and quickly clear up all confusion.

The word, "prayer", subconsciously triggers the feeling of forbiddance, in most people, and rekindles instant recall to remind you about all the times, your requests were allegedly rejected. I started manifesting all of my dreams and desires, *like lady luck*, when I substituted the word, "sayer" for the word, "prayer". The conventional prayer pleads the problem, to the heavens up high, and the sapient sayer settles the specific solution, inside of their being. Believing you receive, right on the spot, whatsoever you say, is the only validation you should ever need, to put you at peace, knowing you shall assuredly receive your request at the perfect hour. Praying the problem repeatedly rises up from disbelief and will warrant why you won't receive your request, unless a sapient sayer, in your circle, is speaking on your behalf, like I did for my father. Feel free to ask trusted family and friends to have faith for you during those times that you feel discouraged, but be sure to specify for them, the solution you are seeking.

Believing "fit for receiving" is activated with, "I AM" affirmations and ascends to the day after Christmas as in; I just got the gift I desired. Remember how when I hung up the phone with my father, I said "Thank you that his ear is clear"? This seven word sentence signifies that I sincerely believe that the problem is a thing of the past and his ear is already clear. You can easily relate to this feeling, by thinking back to a time, when you asked someone special to buy you a particular present for your birthday. It could have been a week before your actual birth date but when they gave you their word that they would come through, with what you wanted, did you not instantly feel like you already got your gift even though it was not physically handed to you yet? You start seeing, in your mind, all the ways you will be enjoying your new novelty, finding yourself feeling fantastic, without actually being in possession of your present. Did I hear an, "oh-yah!" out of you, just now?

That is the surefire feeling you will remember to recall and resort to, every time, you resolve to make anything manifest, in your physical reality. *Right this second* is the only time that realistically exists. Yesterday does not realistically exist, nor does tomorrow. All the power to accomplish anything that you desire is yours to use right now, to turn *dreads into dreams*. When you can place yourself in the PRESENT moment, with the feeling of having already received your "PRESENT", in a previously past moment, and foresee yourself enjoying the experiences that your present entails, for the future days ahead, then nothing in this world will be out of your reach ever again.

You have the right to wake up every day, feeling like it is your birthday, with expectations of enjoying the materialization that matter to you, when these steps become second nature. Start to prepare yourself, by meditating tonight, on all the memories that match the example of the experience about the birthday present, cited above, and get lost in the fantastic feelings that fire up. As we advance, you will learn how to regulate this force to pull in any definite desire you dispatch.

Bringing to Pass Whatsoever Wealth You Wish

For verily I say unto, That whosoever shall say unto this mountain, Be thou removed, and be thou cast into the sea; and shall
not doubt in his heart, but shall believe that those things which
he saith shall come to pass; he shall have whatsoever he saith.
~ Mark 11:23 (K.J.V.) ~

The unrestricted power and permission to call forth whatsoever you wish is completely confirmed in the scripture above. This
passage is not well-know, by the general public, and accounts for
why most people picture that financial freedom is a pipe dream that
only comes true for a select few. The system, put into place by
society, sends people into the working world and provides paying
positions to perform physical tasks. This system is safe, sound and
to be appreciated because most people would not know how to
bounce back or "bank a buck" without it. The only problem with
this set system is that substantial wealth can only be created by
working with our minds and our mouths.

Hard work is to be held in the highest regard when it
springs forth from passion and rewards you with riches that exceed
all of the expenditures you accrue throughout your life. It is horrific
that nearly half of the working world lives "paycheck to paycheck"
but that need not be the case for you. No extra effort is required of
you to radically reverse the direction of your finances, but an open
mind is a must and the willingness, to follow an unfamiliar formula,
is mandatory. Working with your mind and words, then noticing
how your body naturally ends up, at the right place and at the right
time, will take practice but it becomes extremely easy, with continual
use.

The intention of this chapter is to rip the roof right off of your limited beliefs about wealth creation and broaden your horizons regarding the reality of being able to bring to pass, whatsoever wealth you wish. The scripture, from the previous page, is comprised of the 3 essential components that we previously covered and now we can look at them from a higher level, to increase our confidence that **they will work <u>when</u> we execute them:**

Essential Component 1:
"Shall not doubt in his heart"

Essential Component 2:
"Shall believe that those things which he saith shall come to pass"

Essential Component 3:
"Shall have whatsoever he saith"

You can "speak", any amount of money into existence, and when backed by belief, in your heart, you can put your head down on the pillow, at night, *knowing* that it will makes its way into your world.

Notice how nothing more is required of you than to speak something specific; do not doubt…believe those things, you say, will come to pass and YOU SHALL HAVE WHATSOEVER you call forth from your mouth!!!

With your mind, *you* will *decide* the exact income increase, you desire. With your mouth, *you* will *speak* your request, with **<u>absolutely certainty</u>**, that your desire is a done deal, knowing up until the merging moment that your body will be gravitated to the right place and time, for reception.

Notice how nowhere in this power-packed passage, you are being asked to figure out when, where or how it will come to pass?

The need to know who, what, where, when and how poses as a problem for most people. We are pre-programmed, at an early age, to have all the answers in advance but fortunately we possess the power to rise above any habitual thought pattern that could cause us to cancel out our desires. When we really reflect on the fact that we are not responsible to figure out who, what, where, when or how, we should be happier than a kid with an ice cream cone, because the hardest part of the process is not on our shoulders.

Human beings typically tend to be creatures of habit but they are not bound by them in any way whatsoever. Only those that consciously break free from instant recall responses and reactions can seize all the opportunities that surround them. It should be the best news that you have heard all week that this fail-proof formula pardons you from the frustration of figuring out who, what, where, when and how. Those people, who can't push past the need to know precise details to the delivery of their desire, have too much doubt in their heart to make it manifest.

Whenever someone asks me how I think their desire will manifest, the greatest answer I can give them is, "NOW IS HOW". Your mind may trick you into thinking that this formula is hard, until you experience how extra easy it is, by making yourself stick with it for a minimum of one month. The next 30 days is a pinch to pay, compared to all the desires you can call forth, and results will happen, faster than you can imagine, for you to fly through the first few weeks.

There are some people, who can make their belief match their manifestation, in a matter of minutes but more often than not, people habitually hold onto out-of-date beliefs, for dear life.

The first thing you need to ask yourself is, "Could my current beliefs be the real reason for my lack of wealth"? Also ask yourself, "If my current beliefs are already working wonders, in my life, then why am I wasting my time, reading a book about fortunes"?

Since *belief* is like a magic wand and our words spoken with certainty, the *spell*, we are going to spend the next several pages, revolutionizing the way we look at how to bring wealth into our world. This has *nothing to do* with witchcraft or wizardry, and *everything to do* with believing that we possess the power to call forth, any physical manifestation we desire. Much more than mind over matter, belief is a state of being that fluently attracts, into its atmosphere, all the things and experiences that mirror every emotion of faith or fear, from within. We will touch more, on the power of faith and fear, in Chapter 9.

Our society denies its birthright riches, each and every time it brings up the issue of how the economy has gone to hell. Little does society realize that it's not only contributing to the poor conditions of the economy, with it's very words and making it their own reality with this way of thinking, but worst of all, society is squandering away all of its "could-be" breakthroughs. Do you really think that just because an economy is in a depression or recession, there aren't millionaires, being made?

If you are near a computer, with Internet access, I would like for you to set this book aside for 5 minutes, *right now*, and do a search for the term "Millionaires made during The Great Depression". *Can you believe it?* "It's a little known fact that more millionaires were made during The Great Depression than in any other era in U.S. History", according to Sandra S. Simmons, "How to Become a Millionaire During the Next Depression", Article on www.ezinearticles.com. You can see for yourself and believe it or not, but *it is the blatant truth*. Blaming the economy for personal, failing finances is as beneficial as blaming the weatherman for the bad weather that followed his forecast.

Not only are there millions of millionaires but we also have breathing billionaires, occupying our world. It may or may not be your mission to manifest this much money in your lifetime and we will work with your financial freedom figure, in Chapter 15, but we have got to expand your mind, about *abundance*, so to establish a new frame of mind, from which to operate off of.

Most people spend every second of their life, obsessing over money, but it seldom crosses their mind to investigate the make up of money and the unlimited advantages, available for netting more in one week, than most people make in a month. When we act on our desire to explore the deeper depths of wealth; a whole new world of opportunity and prospering probability, opens up.

If you live in the U.S.A., ask anyone you know where money is manufactured, and then, hand over a hundred dollar bill to the person who answers accurately, because they deserve to be rich if they did their research. The Bureau of Engraving and Printing produces all of the U.S.A. paper currency. The Bureau of Engraving and Printing is located in Washington, DC and Fort Worth, TX. If you are ever in either of these areas, you can take a tour and see millions of dollar being printed, right in front of your face.

According to Fun Facts section, on the Bureau of Engraving and Printing's website, www.bep.treas.gov, during the fiscal year 2008, the (BEP) produced approximately 38 million notes a day, with a face value of approximately $629 million. This works out to be billions of dollars, being manufactured each and every month. It is also reported in the Fun Facts section that 95% of the notes printed are issued to replace notes already in, or taken out of circulation. Therefore, approximately 5% of $629 million are added into circulation every day, which produces a surplus of approximately $31 million daily. If we multiply $31 million a day by 251 working days in a year, we become aware that approximately $7.7 billion dollars are added into circulation annually.

In the year 2008 alone, approximately $7.7 billion additional dollars were produced, for distribution. Now sink your teeth into this: According to the Bureau History section, on the (BEP) website, the establishment of the Bureau of Engraving and Printing can be traced as far back as August 29, 1862. Do you realize how much money is moving around our world, and that the sole purpose of manufacturing money is for the benefit of human beings?

Now would be the best time to share with you, one of my "*down to the dollar*" true manifestation stories, to prove that the 3 components work, **when you work them.**

The company I had been working with, for 7 years, decided to relocate to another state. A few of us were asked if we were interested in making the move with them. The relationships in my life are more important to me than money and I love living in New York too much, to leave, so I thanked them for the offer but declined. The timing couldn't have been better because I was starting to become bored with my office job, after doing it for almost a decade, and I had felt a career change coming for quite some time.

As human nature would have it, almost all of the people that cared about me, strongly suggested that I stick with what I know and not take any risks. Reflecting back to when I was a teenager, I came into the knowledge that nobody would ever know me better, than I know myself. Subsequently, I never felt the need to follow in the footsteps of those that I loved, so it was to be expected that I was going to do what *I wanted* to do. In spite of all the precautions, being aimed at me, I whipped out my writing pad and put on my "thinking cap".

After about 2 hours of serious brainstorming, I was settled on the next line of work, I desired to do. I made the definite decision that I would love to be an inside sales representative, responding to incoming customer calls. I would, in no way, make cold calls. My starting salary must be $50K plus commission per sale and I also wrote in my notebook that I would only be willing to travel up to the town of Commack. The memory of that day, when I made these definite decisions, is still very vivid in my mind and I can remember how confident I felt about the position, I custom created. I wrapped my mind, steadily, around this specific sales position, knowing that it would quickly come to pass. In the meantime, I was acutely aware that I couldn't prevent others from worrying about my decision, but I wasn't going to let that stop me from "holding out" for what I wanted.

Within 3 day, I got a phone call from my friend Tracey, who I had not heard from, in over a year. She called, saying that the company, where she worked, was hiring, and that I immediately popped into her head. I wasn't the slightest bit surprised when she informed me that it was an inside sales position, located in Commack, that cold calling was never necessary because the product that they offered was in such high demand and that the starting salary was $50K, along with a very generous commission structure. I met with the owner, the next day, and I started the following week. Can I get a "ka-ching and congratulations"?

All too often, I hear people saying, "What I want is not out there", but the truth of the matter is that it will appear in your world, **when *you* put it out there**. Whatsoever you want will be yours when you believe, without wavering, and that is all there is to it. If you do not doubt in your heart, the manifestation will start. You can have, whatsoever you say, and the power, within, will pave the way.

So shall my word be that goeth forth out of my mouth: it shall not return unto me void, but it shall accomplish that which I please, and it shall prosper (in the thing) whereto I sent it.
~ Isaiah 55:11 (K.J.V.) ~

It is crucial that we monitor our mind and mouth if we truly want to turn it all around. For every one hour we invest into intelligent thinking, and speak, as the authority that we are, over our individual lives, we spare ourselves from weeks of working, out of obligation. Like the scripture on the previous page says, your words **WILL NOT** return unto you, void, *and* **WILL** accomplish that which **YOU** please. There is nothing selfish about being pleased, in every area of your life, as it is every adult's destiny to develop into the authoritative co-creator of their unique universe. You were not born to be other people's puppet or live your life, according to anyone else's expectations. Ultimately, the power, within, will take you anywhere you want to go, as it guides you all along the way, but it's up to you and only you, who must decide the places that are most pleasing.

The effective example, below, will prove to you that busying your body and throwing it into action will never bring about results, the way that *believing* will.

Way back in the day, I thought that owning a Home Based Business was the only way to wealth and after speaking with a well-to-do woman, I talked myself into selling the popular product, Herbalife. I honestly had no interest in learning about the history of the company or the ingredients in the product because my main motivation was all the money I could make. I have come so far, since then, and trust me when I say that I am no longer money motivated but instead, I'm driven, by heart felt desires, which makes ALL the difference, in the world.

My self-made mentor provided me with proof of all the money she was making, every week, giving me the exact game plan she followed, to get these great results. For the next month, I took every action that my mentor carried out, spending more money on advertising, than I could afford, at the time. I made daily phone calls to my mentor and she had no problem, e-mailing me documentation of her daily orders, whenever I would ask her to, because she knew that it would keep me motivated. I did not make a single sale and I knew, back then, why that was.

It was not that I didn't believe in the product or the game plan, because many millionaires were made, from selling Herbalife. My mentor was making a six-figure income, from the comforts of her own home, and she was only promoting the product, part-time. How could it possibly be that two people, taking the same actions, had my mentor, succeeding, while I was failing, miserably?

It all boils down to *belief.* I did not believe I would succeed, whereas my mentor did. My mentor was motivated by how much she believed; that this business was the best fit for her, and so, the money came pouring in...for her. I had no passion for product pushing and though my main motivation was money, I ended up fifteen hundred dollars in debt because I did not believe in what I was doing. I did not believe that I would prosper because, deep down, I desired to stop selling products, as a way of making money. I walked away from this experience, with very valuable insight, and I have been successful, ever since, because I learnt my lesson, the first time around.

There are thousands of ways to make thousands of dollars, every day, which will cross your path as soon as you believe that they exist, while also believing that you will find a perfect fit that pleases you. Did you know that a millionaire averages over $2,500.00 a day? There are millions of people, making this much money, from Monday through Sunday and there is no reason why you can not achieve any financial goal you set for yourself.

Owning a Home Based / Business is only one, out of thousands of ways, to generate wealth. The wisdom, within you, can reveal to you, right now, at least 10 soul satisfying ways for you to manifest the money you desire, *but only after* you take the time to think through a specific figure, that feels right, and not just a "knee-jerk number". In Chapters 12, we will disclose the straightforward steps for tapping into the power, within.

I have come into contact with people, who are making money in the most unusual ways, and love what they do so much that they would do it for free. This guy, Dan, that I know, set up a simple 2-page website and he gets a handful of people to mail him thousands of dollars, every week, with his unknown, cash gifting system. Another friend of mine is buddies with a fellow, who has been making multiple-six-figures, for several years, by getting good at betting on horse races and he is having the time of his life. There also are people, who are turning "trash into cash" and others who are making more money from the "hobbies" that they love, than they did at their day jobs. You will be able to turn your "dreams into dollars", by beginning to believe, ALL things ARE possible and according to YOUR faith, be it done unto you.

Check out this story, about a woman, who pays her way through life by *calling forth* and cashing in on, winning lottery tickets….

If you do an Internet search for "manifest $100,000 in lotto", you will come across the story of a woman, who intended to manifest $100K in 7 weeks. She ended up winning the lotto jackpot, for $100K, 6 ½ weeks after launching her initial intention. This same woman set out to manifest an additional $150K, within 6 months, and low and behold, 6 months later, she won the $200K lotto jackpot! Search for similar stories and you will see for yourself, the endless stream of success, by those people, believing and acting on the power, within themselves.

If you desire it, you can acquire it, in any possible way you wish **but**, YOU *have to believe it to receive it*. You have this power, within yourself, so how soon will you start using it???

The Rich Rewards from Being Your Own Best Friend

If I have lost confidence in myself, I have the Universe against me.
~ Ralph Waldo Emerson (1803-1882) ~

Would you like to know the names of the two thieves who are accountable for all you have lost and lack in this life? Without you even being aware of them, these two clever crooks have managed to sneak in, through the back door, and have been watching every move you make, for years. When you yank them, out of hiding, with your awareness, they have no other choice but to flee to a far away place, where their cover will not be blown.

Over to your left is evil enemy #1, who goes by the name of *fear* and over to your right, is his perfect partner in crime, evil enemy # 2, who you can call *uncertainty*. At the lowest point in your life, these two tag-teamed you and pick pocketed your most precious God given gift...**certainty**. *Life, without certainty*, is like the sky, without the sun. You stop seeing clearly and constantly sense that something significant is missing.

We are all victims of having our *certainty*, snatched from us, and yet, here we are, all on scavenger hunts, in hot pursuit of making more money, to fill this void. An abundance of money and an overflow of every other good thing will "tidal wave into your world" but *ONLY* when you are wise enough to realize that the buried treasure you seek, is inside of you. *Certainty* contains the code to every seemingly impossible combination. It rolls out the red carpet, in the right direction, leading you to your, "Oscar outcome", every time. The phenomenal fact is that your *certainty* has always remained intact but has been held hostage, by fear and uncertainty. Today is the day we will set your *certainty*, free, and give you an eagle eye view of all the wealth that has been waiting for you.

Has it never been brought to your attention before, how brilliantly the creator of this world brings everything into being? The creator of this world is beyond description but can be thought of as *infinite intelligence* and *endless energy* that mass produces one magnificent manifestation after another, out of invisible space, from the mighty mechanics of certainty. "Let there be" is allegedly the subtle, starting statement to every earthly creation. It makes no difference if you believe in the Big Bang Theory or subscribe to organized outlooks on life, because common sense and careful analysis, would agree that only something of a certain nature could create all of the captivating scenery that surrounds us.

*We are unfolding something **HUGE** here so stick with me for a minute...*

Could you picture an all-powerful creator, pleading to the universe, "Please, please, pretty please, let there be a palm tree"? Far from it and more like, "Let there be a palm tree, right there, in that spot". *Certainty* does not doubt or force anything into being but simply knows that if it is spoken, then it must in fact, manifest. It is documented that the creator calls forth things that be not as if they already exist and every specification spontaneously appears. We are also informed, whether we choose to believe it or not, that we were made in the identical image and likeness of the creator, with the built-in blueprint to create, in the same exact manner.

Be brutally honest with yourself...do you not doubt most of the decisions you make and question almost every action you take or do you constantly get complimented on the exuberant *certainty* you exhibit?

There is a switch inside of you that will instantly turn on *total confidence*, when you make the firm decision to always act on the same advice that you would bestow to your best friend.

Don't you find it frustrating when one of your friends comes to you for advice and you provide them with the perfect solution that will permanently solve their situation, but they never follow through? Instead, they keep coming to you, week after week, with the same problem, hoping that you will come up with another way to permanently solve their problem. Doesn't it make you want to shake your friend, by the shoulders, because you can clearly see how happy they would be, if only they did as you suggested. You give them one great alternative after another and then, comes the day when you finally realize that they haven't taken any action because *they want someone to do it for them!!!*

Before you go getting yourself worked up about all the times your friends have ignored your brilliant advice, that would have surely given them the satisfaction they sought, *ask yourself, why* **you** *do not act in accordance with your own advice?* You can permanently solder your self-confidence, by writing down all of your dreams, and asking yourself, "What advice would I give my good friend that would get them all of these things"? It is amazing when we discover that all of the answers were inside of us, all along, but we never approach our heart felt desires or problems, the way we are willing to do, for our family and friends.

When you flip the switch from being your own worst enemy, to being your own best friend, the universe that is engineered to reveal your inward reflections, on the outside, will then, in return, project all the pleasing experiences you now expect to physically, come forth. I would like to provide you with a powerful new way to start seeing yourself, and the impersonal way that the universe works, to make anything you say, subsequently manifest. Visualize yourself, standing at the edge of a mountain top, and screaming the words, "I Love You!!", out loud. What do you think the ensuing echo back will be? "I love you"…"I love you…"I love you". Now, picture yourself, screaming the words, "I hate you!!" The mirroring universe will justly, echo back, "I hate you"…"I hate you…"I hate you".

There is nothing unfair about the universe, treating you the way you treat yourself, and what you can expect is, when you start feeling honored about *who and all that you are*, **you will be honored**, in the outer world. You may have been thinking badly about yourself, for years, believing that you're nothing special, but from this second, forward, it will reward you richly to say nothing but the very best things, about yourself. Your whole life and every experience you have encountered, has been preparing you to be your own best friend. The person, who becomes his / her own best friend, will not flinch if the rest of the world walks out, because they know how to call forth, constant companionship and create a lifestyle that outshines the old one.

Confidence can not be faked, which explains why most of the media hype books, about manifesting, leave their loyal readers, feeling like failures. You can *think* you are confident, but if you *do not feel* confident, **nothing will change**. You can *think* to yourself, every day for the next 5 years, "the corvette is coming", "the corvette is coming", "the corvette is coming" but until you *feel certain* that you already own the corvette, you will be driving around, in the car you currently use, until the day it breaks down. *Knowledge*, that strikes a nerve, forcing you to dig beneath your surface self, in search of discovering the true sovereign self that you are, can not be compromised. The day you get that glimpse of your true identity and all the magical qualities you possess, only then will you know how to consciously create your exemplary life.

I AM the LORD, and there is none else, there is no God beside
me: I girded you, though you have not known me.
~ Isaiah 45:5 (A.K.J.V.) ~

The charismatic creator of this colorful world is attached to you, at all times, but very few are aware of this fact. The Dictionary.com definition for "girded" is: to bind, encircle, enclose, fasten, secure and surround. Like it or not, there is no inch on this earth, where you can escape from creative energy. This also very much means that every ounce of your body and being, is infused with creative energy. Did the passage, on the previous page, not also start off with the words, "I AM"? Well, here they are again! Has it dawned on you yet, on how they pertain to you, personally? You are always intimately involved, when you say the words, I AM. You are never taking about anyone else, when you say, *I AM*, are you? For example, "I am sick", "I am great", "I am wealthy", "I am healthy", "I am the best", "I am an idiot" etc. These two highly creative words are mistakenly taken for granted, by most people. You can use these two words to transcend your self-image and station in life, whenever you wish, even though most people feel like they are locked into to their current conditions.

> Let the weak say I am strong.
> ~ Joel 3:10 (K.J.V.) ~

If there is anything you have been saying about yourself, that you desire to be different or altogether opposite, then by all means, replace it right now. If, in the past, you found it difficult to continue in your newfound faith, waiting for the replacement reality to reveal itself, then fasten tight to the following fact I AM about to disclose to you. Have you ever heard someone use the expression, "I have been running around like a chicken, with his head cut off"? Once a chicken has had its head cut off, its body can run around, alive, for up to the distance of 2 football fields, before dying. On Wikipedia.com, there is documentation of a chicken that lived 18 months, after having his head cut off, who is known as "Mike", the headless chicken.

If your resolve is strong, around receiving your new reality right away, it will be but a short distance for the old reality to die and the desired reality to take its place. On the other hand, if your resistance to receiving your new reality is stronger than your resolution, you will, undisputedly, keep the old life alive, longer.

In chapter 15, we will go over in distinct detail how to strengthen your resolve and release resistance.

Through faith we understand, that the worlds were framed by the word of God, so that things which are seen were not made of things which do appear.
~ Hebrews 11:3 (K.J.V.) ~

For the greater portion of your life, you have based your identity on your body, and more than likely, you made up your mind about who you are, according to your physical appearance. Then again, perhaps you've based your identity upon the opinions of others, in regards to your appearance. Things which are seen, (*Body*) were not made from things which do appear; meaning that the unseen source (*Spirit*), from which you came, is your true ipseity, and your body that now appears as a physical object, sprang forth, from the invisible side of your self. Our minds are also invisible, but we are well aware that we have one. The physical aspect of who you are is but a speck, compared to the unlimited size of your spirit. Your mind is second place, to spirit, in terms of the power it possesses, so why is it then that we believe, it is our bodies that bring to pass, the physical objects and outcomes we desire?

Watch how much this all makes sense and get ready to finally apply the formula correctly, for any designated and desirable outcome...

No Seed (Spirit) = No Flower (Body)
No Soil (Mind) = No Flower (Body)
Seed (Spirit) but no soil (Mind) = No Flower (Body)
Soil (Mind) but no seed (Spirit) = No Flower (Body)
Seed (Spirit) + Soil (Mind) = Flower (Body)

In this instant, we are going to free ourselves, from the inaccurate theory of the traditional, "Body-Mind-Spirit" philosophy and celebrate this weekend, for having correctly spun it around to the, "Spirit-Mind-Body" position, where it rightfully belongs!!! To break out of that "barely getting by" mentality, we have to do things differently.

The desires of our heart are the seeds, given to us by *spirit*. *Desire* rooted in *certainty* is like a strawberry seed, planted in soil. The strawberry seed (*Spirit*) contains the code for producing a physical strawberry bush (*Body*) before it is planted in soil (*Mind*). There is zero pressure on the soil to calculate how it is going to make a strawberry bush, out of the inserted seed. The *spirit* created the mathematical code to everything in existence, and scientists dedicate their entire lives, deciphering these codes, without taking credit for the creation of these genius combinations. The soil (*Mind*) simply accepts the seed (*Spirit*) and the flower (*Body*) appears. *Don't you find it fascinating, that a single seed has the power to produce a multiple harvest?* The ten-fold return principle also applies to our deep seated desires, providing us with proof and assurance that the power, within, is *"able to do exceedingly abundantly above all that we ask or think!!!"*

Your body was brought to life, precisely, in the same way as everything else. All that you are was deeply desired in the spirit realm. Your unique awareness agreed to and accepted this custom combination then your body became born. The development of your mind was dependant on the adults, around you, when you were a youngling, but now you are mature enough to manage your own mind. When we were younger, we could get away with blaming the adults, around us, for our actions or hold them accountable for not getting what we wanted. But as adults ourselves now, **no one can keep us** *from creating the life we love, outside of our own minds.* You are free to hold on tightly to the mind that was molded for you, by others, **or** you can master your own mind, from this moment, forward, and only accept seeds, in your soil, that manifest your favorite arrangement of flowers.

If you are in favor of yourself, the whole universe will work in your favor. However, if you are against yourself, then you will feel like the whole world is against you. Having heard that you were custom created, out of deep desire from the spirit realm, and that no one on this planet has the same finger prints as you or similar Spirit-Mind-Body combination that you do, what words will make you accept that you are already absolutely awesome?

The only reason why you are not already where you want to be and enjoying the experiences you dream about daily is because *CERTAINTY* had been forgotten about, up to now.

How can one be certain, in a world inundated with doubt, fear and worry?

One by one, we will all be called, to reclaim our *certainty* and **your time has arrived today!!!** You are already half way to home base, and by the last sentence of this book, your *certainty* should be completely restored to its unscathed state. For the time being, while everyone else blindly believes that barrels of money is the answer to their problems, would YOU at least be willing to see through this mirage and consider that *certainty* is what every one in this world is TRULY after, but they have become too hypnotized, by false fears, to realize this quality as being the substance they seek. *Certainty*, not only can call forth big bank balances and all the other objects of your desire, but you will also never be one of those people who can't sleep at night, in fear that one day they will lose everything. *Fear* transforms everything, from GOOD *to* GONE, over time, but *certainty* steadily turns GOOD *into* GREAT.

Repeat to yourself, as many times as it takes to override opposing beliefs, that *certainty* IS the substance of all things hoped for and that ALL things ARE possible!!!

You no longer have to phone a friend and ask them if "xyz" is possible because you are building the belief that all things are possible, and therefore, the answer is always an astounding "YES!!!" As comforting as human nature finds getting verbal validation from others, the truth is that unless the person you are consulting, "thinks outside of the box", you will more than likely get "shot down, like a duck". Here is an excellent example…on several occasions, when someone would ask me what I wanted to be, when I got older; my firm answer was always, "I want to be an author". After stating this desire, with absolutely certainty, one person replied, "You should be a Teacher", while another person said to me, "You should be an Attorney", and someone else suggested, "You should be a Nurse"??? It used to make my head spin, having people ask me what I wanted to be, only to have them insistently recommend an alternative vocation, so remotely different from my earnest desire.

You don't have to take what others say, to heart, when they are so, "off-base", but at the same time, don't put yourself in the position, of being detoured from your desires.

There is no better time, than now, to place yourself back at the top of your priority list, where you've belonged, all along, and make sustained *certainty* your # 1 mission.

Let's start to lock in **your** *certainty,* by going back to the "Spirit-Mind-Body" sequence.

Seed (Spirit) + Soil (Mind) = Flower (Body)

Consider the simple steps that a Gardener goes through, to cultivate his crops. **He is inspired** to grow a beautiful garden, in his backyard, for the first time in years. **He is determined**, to get back into gardening, and takes the time to envision the landscape design, he desires to manifest. **He immediately becomes aware** of the number of seeds he needs and the specific assortment of seeds, after his layout, is finalized. He inserts the seeds into the soil, and **the thought that his flowers won't flourish, never crosses his mind.** He waters the garden area, mid morning and early evening, with **expectancy that any given day** his garden will be in full bloom. His excitement increases, each time he returns to water the area, because all of the flowers grow bigger, by the day. Before he knows it, his eyes are feasting **on the physical replica** of his recently, imaginary and invisible idea.

This is the easiest formula to follow and it can only fail to produce physical results if the soil (*Mind*) is not properly prepared. When we replicate the same, simple steps that the gardener actively applies, then we are guaranteed to get the physical manifestation that we predetermine as well.

Most people are not aware of the 3 bullet points, listed below, or they instantly reject them because these *advantage points* threaten their life long belief that manifesting has to be hard. However, because **YOU** are now armed with the awesome knowledge and power of *certainty*, you are able to appreciate the value of these advantage points. Start applying these steps, as soon as possible, and all of your desires will be physically placed on your path, for the purpose of pure pleasure:

1. The gardener not only **takes the time to select the specific seed,** he desires to manifest, but he **does not doubt,** for a second, that the seed knows how to make it all happen, and all he has to do is insert the seed into the soil. It does not matter if you never looked at it, like this before, but the truth of the matter is that **your desires are seeds that contain the complete code for fruition.** If you desire a black pair of Timberland boots, the desire for this specific set carries with it, the perfect plan to obtain those exact boots. You have to choose if you will accept the seed or cast it aside. If the same desire keeps coming up, that means you keep casting it aside, and if it has not manifested physically, then that means you worried yourself with,

"How much it was going to cost?" and "How on earth am I going to pull this off?" **STOP** throwing away your seeds by concerning yourself with *HOW* it will happen and *WHAT* it will cost. Prepare the soil (*Mind*), by selecting the specific seed **YOU want** to be planted. When I desired my Movado watch, I instantly "accepted the seed" and I didn't worry about dollars, days or an outline.

2. After the gardener inserts the seed into the soil, the thought that his flowers might not or will not flourish **NEVER** crosses his mind. *Why* do we worry, the way we do, and *why* do we doubt that we will never get what we want??? Little did we realize, until now, that our doubt *IS* the very reason why we WILL NOT get what we want. You can have your heart set on anything you desire, but if you don't think you will get it, then you are right and *you won't get it*. We must do what the gardener does, which is **KNOWING** that once the seed is in the soil, we **actually believe that we have already received our outcome**, while waiting, with excited anticipation, for the final culmination.

3. The gardener doesn't let a day go by where he isn't **watering his garden area and expecting that any day** now he will have his bountiful harvest. After our minds are made up, we will be required to water them, with adoring thoughts, anticipating all the enjoyment that is to come our way. Every day, we will be pleased with our present progress, **expecting a full fledge manifestation, at anytime**. As you can now see, from the way the gardener goes about it, expectancy isn't about forcing ourselves to believe but rather, **free flowing *knowing***.

You have just been given the keys to the Kingdom. Take all the time you need to study these steps and allow yourself to start taking your desires, out of the draw. As soon as you have your soil (*Mind*) properly prepared, the formula will be waiting for you, ready to begin blossoming, all of your dream schemes.

Fearless Fortunes and Apology Free Abundance

For God hath not given us a spirit of fear; but of power, and of love, and of a sound mind.
~ 2 Timothy 1:7 (K.J.V.) ~

I wish someone would have spoon fed me this scripture when I was a child because I could have avoided the painful period of my adult life where I became paralyzed by fear and pushed away every golden opportunity presented to me. I am grateful now, for having gone through that tumultuous time in my life, because it forced me to face *fear*, head-on, while acquiring the awareness that *fear*, blindsides even the best of us. I further learned that *fear* tests us, seeing if we will fight for our right to reign or if we will blindly accept, being burdened by worry, until our dying day.

Allow me to point out that we are officially half way through the book, and after we get through this chapter, the rest of the journey is going to be a real joy ride. I have made it my mission, to help you properly prepare your mind for momentous manifesting, and the issue, we are about to address, is too important to ignore. If you were to decide to do nothing with this book, other than free your mind from *fear*, then that would be enough, to have everything begin to unfold in your favor and that is why we will not skip this section. I invite you to grasp hold of my hand, while we work through this final, uncomfortable feeling and know that going forward, we will be blazing into the sunlight like a car driving out of a dark tunnel.

The universal unconscious myth is that *fear* must exist in everyone's mind, as a survival mechanism, as it keeps us safe, from being sneak attacked. In fact, most of us have no idea, of the extent and extraordinary power, this mental conditioning has had on us. The truth is, most people do not know that they have a choice, having been brainwashed to believe that *fear* is as necessary as the air we breathe. In all actuality, fear has never been, nor ever will be, embedded into our true nature, but that does not mean our individual minds will know that we must stop this imposter, from taking over our territory. Regardless of who your parents were or place of your birth, you were born with personal power, unconditional love and a sound mind. None of these gifts are gone; they wait, silently in the stillness of your being, to be accepted and used by your developed awareness.

Fear, in itself, is not a bad thing, when talking in terms of haunted Halloween houses and "Friday The 13th" movies. It is when we *identify* with *fear*, believing that we were born into it, is when our lives transform from fairy tale to nightmare. A good friend of mine used to get such a kick out of hiding behind the counter, whenever I walked by, catching me off guard and busting out hysterical from the frightened look on my face. I fell for my friend's trap, every time, making me laugh just as hard as her.

There is nothing wrong with using *fear* as a form of fascinating entertainment, if horror flicks happen to be your favorite means of amusement, but if you let fear govern your life and dictate your decisions, like most people, do then you can "kiss your personal power, goodbye". Letting *fear* take the driver's seat and putting one's personal power, in the backseat, is as life-threatening as allowing a little child to do the driving instead of a licensed adult. The time has come to put *fear*, in its proper place, and permanently cast it out of our households.

For the thing which I greatly feared is come upon me, and that
which I was afraid of is come unto me.
~ Job 3:25 (K.J.V.) ~

Fear is *faith* that things will not work out or take a turn for the worst, as opposed to believing that things will work out for the best. Did we not discover, a few chapters back, that according to our faith be it done unto us? *Fear* **and** *faith* are both beliefs.

The secret to living a sensational life lies in applying simple wisdom that teaches you how to "starve your *fears*" and "feed your *faith*". We can start to starve our fears to death by believing that we **were not given** a *spirit of fear*, to begin with. The next thing we need to acknowledge is that if we continue to believe that we will be vulnerable to attack, without fear, helping to keep us "on our toes", then we completely miss the point that our *fear* is the very substance that creates our crushing outcome. The thing, I greatly feared, has come upon me, because I greatly feared it. If I did not greatly fear it, it could not have come upon me.

Let me add, at this point, that it is not your fault if you are filled with unconscious *fears*. *Fear* comes from our conditioning, but as intellectual adults, we are responsible to examine our root assumptions about *fear* and put it under the microscope, to expose its nothingness. Not only will all *fear* and apprehension vanish, when we boldly turn it over to truth, but we can quickly restore all that has been taken from us, with a ten-fold return.

> There is no fear in love; but perfect love cast out fear: because fear hath torment. He that fears is not made perfect in love.
> ~ 1 John 4:18 (A.K.J.V.) ~

Are you wondering why I have been bombarding you with nothing but biblical scripture since Chapter 6? I can assure you that we will be weaning ourselves off of scriptures, shortly, but with this most recent war, that has embroiled our nation, we are all awakening to the realization that the root of our fighting and *fear* is revolved around religion. God does not need us to fight for His honor because He is infinitely indestructible and nor would he ever blame us, for having to physically defend ourselves, when we are forced into combat. We have all heard that "God is love" and as indicated above, perfect love has the power to cast out *fear*. This last line also calls to our attention that if we constantly feel fearful, then we must have been gravely misinformed, about God. We have been living in fear, for far too long, and we can deactivate it, as we would any other deadly bomb, when we backtrack to its original religious roots.

Do you go to bed at night, apologizing for all the mistakes you made, throughout the day or do you dwell on all the things, you love about your life?

Do you *fear* dying, because your soul could end up in hell, or do you know, deep down, that the heavens miss you so much and count down the days for your return?

Are you afraid of becoming really rich and "set for life" because you believe that your soul will be sent straight to hell if you do?

Are you afraid that if you were to come into wealth, that other people would "guilt you" into giving them, your good fortune purely out of obligation, instead of you, deciding who you desire you bless out of the goodness of your heart?

Do you worry, every day of the week that you could lose your job and everything else you worked hard for, your whole life?

Are you afraid that if you quit the job you hate, that the next one could be worst, so safer to tough it out where you are or **do you know** that the door to your dream job is wide open and waiting for you to walk through?

Are you afraid of being alone, and you would rather remain in an unhappy relationship than free yourself, to find a partner that makes your spirit sing?

All of the frightening examples, above, are "hand-me-down" *fears*, brought on by other people!!!

If one or more of the fears, from the previous page, thunder through your mind daily, along with a dozen other unnoted fears, you should be happy to hear that there is a flawless solution. The antidote that I am about to share with you will put your mind at ease, establishing a very simple, yet effective, self sustaining belief system. Consider what these 3 little words can do for you, when you absorb them, for all they are worth...**Stellar Self Value.** If *fear* continues to haunt you, then it is clear that you have yet to comprehend how very valuable you are and just *how much power you have*, at your finger tips. Unlike the fearful person, who consistently fails to act or make decisions, until backed against a wall, the person who makes stellar self value, their central station, never wrestles with right or wrong and has no problem, making split second decisions.

My own mother couldn't help but constantly question me about the condemnation aspects of the Bible because it was drilled into her head, at an early age. Many of my like minded friends continue to come to me, with conflicting beliefs that give them grief, and that was more than enough motivation for me to give birth to this book. As I write to you, my revered reader, I speak to you in the same style that I speak to all those, who I hold dear to my heart, attempting to erase all the erroneous beliefs that discourage you, from making your dreams come true.

Do an online search for "Facts about the Bible" and self study all the details that went into the creation of our sacred text. You will come to discover that the Bible was written by over 40 different authors, over a period of approximately 1,500 to 1,600 years, which averages out to be roughly 45 generations in gap. It is documented, according to www.allaboutgod.com, that there are 1,189 chapters in the Bible; 929 chapters comprise the Old Testament and only 260 are contributed to the New Testament. The beginning of the Bible dates back to 1400 B.C. and is estimated to have ended, around 100 A.D.

I spent an entire year, in my early twenties, studying the scriptures, after a devout Christian co-worker, slandered me because I was living with my boyfriend, before marriage. We had already been living together, for 3 years, with never a doubt about our decision to cohabit, when my co-worker confronted us, with her attempt to point out "the error of our ways". It was a blessing in disguise that one judgmental comment, from a Christian, sent me on my search for answers because I cleared my conscience, before my 21st Birthday and I have been carefree, ever since, possessing the ability to tune out all criticisms that come, from other people. I also kid you not, when I inform you that, a little less than a year later, this very same co-worker moved in with her boyfriend, before marriage. We have all failed to practice what we preach, at one time or another and therefore, as far as I am concerned, my co-worker is completely pardoned.

1 Judge not, that ye not be judged. **2** For with what judgment ye judge, shall ye be judged: and with what measure ye mete, it shall be measure to you again.
~ Matthew 7:1-2 (K.J.V.) ~

The last thing you should concern yourself about is what other people think about you or how you choose to live your life because, like a boomerang, their judgments will return to them, faster than they can catch them. **No one**, in this world, has the right to pass judgment on you but if you insist on judging yourself or others, then please be prepared for it to backfire. The protestors that force their beliefs on others and infringe on human rights, will have to learn the hard way, the day they wake up, only to find the universe, aiming all those arrows, back at them. You will forever be free from judgment when you become too busy creating the life you love and implementing the attitude of "I could really care less what others think of me". Also, it's important that you realize that anyone who would pass judgment on you is merely attempting to avoid addressing their own inner issues. You'll find that it is better to be compassionate towards these people, than waste your personal power on the unproductive undertakings of others.

A life, free from **all fear,** is not only possible but it's proven to be preordained, in the scripture that says God did not give us a *spirit of fear.* From now on, feel free to "brush off" anyone who uses fear, in any form, against you and your loved ones.

The fear of growing old is another unconscious apprehension, in the minds of most people, and we need to nip that in the bud, by realizing that the *spirit,* inside of you, does not age, ever. The ability to create anything you desire does not expire at any age. If you are alive, at the age of 88, you still possess the inner power to call forth things that be not as if they were and according to your faith, it will be done unto you. Do you see daytime television's sweetheart, Susan Lucci, slowing down now that she is in her 60's or have you realized that this remarkable woman is never going to stop living life to the fullest? Take your mind off of your age and turn your attention to that incredible, ageless power that relentlessly works within you, at all times.

Now, going back to where we left off, regarding Bible facts, emphasizing once again, how it was written by over 40 different authors, many moons ago, are you ready to begin appreciating it from a refreshing point of view?

The Bible is said to have been inspired by the Holy Spirit. Does the Holy Spirit not live inside of each and every one of us, according to the book of Corinthians? If this is true, then do we not all receive our inspiration, from the same source, including the authors of our generation?

Have you ever read a non-fiction book, in which you absolutely agreed with everything the author had to share with you or did you have a difference of opinion, on a couple of occasions? Now, borrow 40 different books, written by 40 different authors, from the spiritual section of your local library and let me know if you absolutely agree with everything that each author has to share. Keep in mind that you are bound to come across one conflict of opinion after another, between all of these books. This can explain the reason for all of the contradictions that we come across, in the Bible.

I have read thousands of books, written by hundreds of different authors, and I have yet to find two books, that are anything alike. Many of my favorite books offer outlooks that I do not agree with, but I only apply the information that helps me to achieve the outcome, I am after. You have got to learn how to take what you like, while leaving the rest. If something inside of you says, "I do not agree with this", then that is a clear indication that the information you came across, does not pertain to you, but will be beneficial to someone else. If something inside of you says, "This sits very well with me", then that piece of information was intended to speak to your spirit. No one can make you fill your mind with passages from the Bible that are causing you conflict. In the same way, you would never allow the owner of a public buffet to tell you what foods you can and can not fill up your plate with. **Always** feel free, to pick the passages that make your spirit sing, and give other people the freedom to pick their own passages, even if they go with the ones that make them miserable.

Neither shall they say, See here! or, See there! for, behold, the
kingdom of God is within you.
~ Luke 17:21 (A.K.J.V.) ~

I do not doubt that the Bible was inspired by the Holy Spirit
but that is a personal "opinion" and the truth remains that the 1,189
chapters in the Bible are realistically a compilation of forty plus
other people's "opinions". Do you spend your leisure time with
people who bring out the best in you or do you surround yourself
with people who put you down? In that case, wisdom would
declare that you not spend your time on scriptures that destroy your
self esteem. *The kingdom of God is within you*, more so than these
authors, who you have looked up to as the leading authority over
your spiritual life. But again, make note that *the true intention, of the
Bible, was meant to teach you how to branch off and become confident enough to
eventually start searching your own heart for answers.* You can stop fearing
that any action you take, in this lifetime, will be held against you in
an afterlife because **God did not give you a spirit of fear**. If
anything, look at the afterlife, through the eyes of the late John
Milton, such that, "Death is the golden key that opens the palace of
eternity", and not the gates of hell.

The mind in its own place and in itself can make a Heaven of
Hell, a Hell of Heaven.
~ John Milton (1608–1674) ~

Your mind is your kingdom and it is entirely up to you to
decide if your guests will be friend or foe. You are under no
obligation to let the hellish opinions of others take up occupancy in
your domain. Albert Einstein did not hand his mind over to
another human being, to bring out his brilliance, and neither should
you. You are just as free, as Aristotle and Oprah Winfrey, to think
the greatest of thoughts that let your life take flight!!!

One more major oversight, made by most people, in regards to the Bible, is that they lock onto all of the punishment passages from the Old Testament, failing to receive the full forgiveness, offered in the New Testament. The Bible is broken down into two distinct parts to help us humans understand the origin of our negative thinking and then provides us with proof that it is not only possible to become positive thinkers but is expected of all of us, as our minds mature. The negative thinking, that dominates this world, was already addressed and correctly rectified by the creator, long before we entered the earth. When we open our eyes to the fact that the New Testament came *after* the Old Testament, we can rightfully accept that our salvation was settled from the get-go and instantly break free, from any future self inflicted condemnation.

The only thing we have to fear is fear itself.
~ Franklin D. Roosevelt (1882-1945) ~

You were born fearless!!! You were given the ultimate gift of power, love and sound mind, enabling you to bring all of your desires to pass in this lifetime. If it makes your heart skip a beat to manifest a million dollars, then stop apologizing for your desire and start preparing your mind, for it to manifest. There is no reason why you can not become a millionaire, like the millions of others who have, before you, if that is what you truly desire. However, just as they came to believe that this status was possible, making their desire, their reality, you too must begin to believe that this status is 100% possible, for you a well.

If you have no interest in being a millionaire but do desire to live comfortably, for the rest of your life, then you can bring that exact experience to come about, by committing to the belief that it is possible. *Nothing is impossible* and the power to bring it to pass is inside of you, even if you live to be 122, as in the case of Jeanne Calment, who passed away in 1997. *All things are possible* to him that believes and the ability to believe is woven within our being.

Our beliefs are a lot like an alluring and sticky fly trap that dangles down from a ceiling. In the same way that flies are effortless drawn to the tape, it holds true for us, such that our desires are drawn to us. The fly trap never fears that the flies won't come and now we can be fearless to call forth our apology free fortunes.

Winning Over the World with an Attractive Attitude

He that falls in love with himself will have no rivals.
~ Benjamin Franklin (1706-1790) ~

Your attitude definitely does determine your altitude in life and fortunately for us, it is the one thing in this world that we have complete control over. The people who made their millions, during the Great Depression, adjusted their attitudes accordingly and benefited all across the board. There *is nothing in this world you can not claim* when you take your attention off other people's attitudes and work on making your own mind magnetic.

When you take the time to understand the way our world works and learn how to effortlessly handle everyone you come into contact with **you will attract** good fortune, from every direction. *The long lost secret to success is that you can never control another person's actions or attitude but by controlling your own, you can subconsciously influence everyone and everything around you.* There is nothing but disappointment to be gained, by trying to change other people, not to mention that we do not have the right to try to change any one when we were all born with the free will to act as we wish and be who we are.

Be different than everyone else, by starting to accept other people, exactly as they are, and watch how many people will go out of their way to help you because they feel appreciated and respected in your presence. The first step to winning over the world, with an attractive attitude, starts with *accepting yourself* in every single sense. You may have a handful or perhaps hundreds of hang ups that you would like to improve about yourself, but there is nothing you can possibly do to make the true being inside of you any more perfect than it already is right this moment. You are as great as you are ever going to be, and by embracing that, today, your world **will start** turning around, by tomorrow.

Ye are of God, little children, and have overcome them: because
greater is he that is in you, than he that is in the world.
~ 1 John 4:4 (K.J.V.) ~

Everybody, blessed with eyesight, can see all of the struggling and suffering in our world, but the power to come out on top is inside of every last one of us. We were trained to base our beliefs about the world, according to what we see with our eyes, but eyesight was established for the sole purpose of enjoying the view of all the wonders that are around us. As adults, we are responsible to retrain our brain and *realize that the power, within, can overcome anything we dislike* in our outer world but we must stop being filled with fear, from what we witness with our eyes.

Those, less fortunate, suffering with diverse disadvantages, possess just as much personal power as you do and no one can convince them to tap into it until they express the desire to be taught. Like the old saying goes, "Give a man a fish; you have fed him for today. Teach a man to fish; and you have fed him for a lifetime". Continue to contribute, in any way you choose, with the awareness that whoever you help possesses the same greatness as you, and in return, your own personal power will most surely, multiply, with each encounter.

The most powerful way we can help those, who have lost all hope, is by believing in ourselves and allowing our light to shine so bright, that others can't help but notice. When we ignite our own inner light, we are then able to activate the light inside of other people, without the use of words, the same way that we set off a motion sensor light, by walking in front of it. Without any action on your part, other than loyally believing in yourself, the power, within, *will awaken* in everyone, you come into contact with, *even if* neither of you are aware that it is taking place.

Don't ask what the world needs. Ask what makes you come
alive, and go do it. Because what the world needs is people who
have come alive.
~ Dr. Howard Thurman (1899-1981) ~

You are not responsible to bring out the best in others but it
will be impossible not to, when you at your very best, pursuing your
passions and living life on your own terms, to the fullest. *The only
thing that has stopped you from getting started is fear of failure and fear of
succeeding*, over others. Say out loud in your strongest voice possible,
"*Failure is not an option*" and "*I will inspire everyone who meets me by
making all of my dreams come true*". When you make the definite
decision that failure is not an option and realize how important your
individual success is, to the rest of the world, the power, within, will
plow over any obstacles that could come up.

The people of this world are infatuated with athletes and ce-
lebrities because they inspire others to tap into their personal
potential and prove that one can create a lifestyle, filled with fun
festivities, simply by believing in yourself. Fame is not necessary for
manifesting fortunes but, figuring out what you are passionate about
and then, fearlessly taking the first step, by yourself, will put you on
the pathway to your dream world. By all means, *you are welcome to
invite* anyone you love, to join in on all the adventures, but *you can not
expect* anyone else to encourage you and support you, every step of
the way. The highest degree of self-confidence can only be obtained by daring to manifest your dreams, all by yourself, as your
family and friends may not have the free time to assist you. Always
remember though, **the power, within, will** place the appropriate
people, on your path, whenever helping hands or master minds are
needed.

Some people have the subconscious fear that wealth will
change them in a negative way and are afraid that the people they
love will leave them. Nothing could be further from the truth and

everyone you have close connections with, will be more motivated than ever, to unearth their own deep seated desires. You do not have start purchasing memberships at the local country clubs and abandon the activities you presently love, when you manifest more wealth. Having more money will enable you to do _whatever you desire, whenever you desire and with whomever you desire_. You will also be in a position, to "pick up the tab", for family and friends, when generosity hits your heart. Nothing about you or your life will change in a negative way whatsoever and the people, you care about, will not act any differently towards you. Chances are, you will be a much happier person to be around and your peace of mind will rub off on others.

There will always be people out there who are envious of anyone, demonstrating any degree of wealth, but this is _not to be feared_ nor looked at, in the negative sense. Those people, who appear to dislike you, due to jealousy, are silently stating that you are an answer to their prayer. They are too afraid to approach you, to ask how they, too, can create what you have, because it just might make them as happy as it has made you. However, not only will you soon have all the answers for them, but imagine how many people you can inspire, by having the ability to understand their unspoken intentions and taking 10 minutes, out of your time, to share with them, what you now know. You could even consider starting your own consulting company, charging $100.00 an hour, custom-creating "blueprints", tailored around your dedicated clients' desires and dreams or design a website that does all the work for you. This is the going rate that people are happy to pay, for a one hour session with a reputable hypnotherapist, psychologist and psychic who _confidently_ offer their services, to others.

From firsthand experience, I am a firm believer that when we eliminate the enemies, living inside us, there will not be nor can be, enemies on the outside. The same can be said for _self belief_. _When we believe in ourselves_ and fall in love, with all that we are, not only will *others naturally believe in us* but we unconsciously confirm, that it is safe for them to do the same.

You place yourself in a very powerful and profitable position, when you learn how to interpret other people's true intentions, by putting yourself in their shoes and spend the extra thirty seconds it takes to pick up on their genuine agenda. It will not take much practice, on your part, and soon you will find yourself generating several, solid solutions, to people's exasperating problems. You will have earned every right to set a fair price, that is beneficial to both you and the people you provide valuable insight to, but more importantly, it will make your heart melt, when you see how admirable, most human beings are, when the weight of the world has been lifted off of their chest.

It does not make a dent of difference if you are introverted or extraverted. *The wealth of this world will be distributed to those* that make the definite decision to get their "piece of the pie" even if they do not have an outgoing "bone in their body". Never forget that by **YOUR BELIEF**, be it done unto you. There are thousands of incredible opportunities, designed to increase your income without interacting with other people, face-to-face, or over the phone. *However,* when you unleash the understanding on how your fellow human beings have been predisposition to behave; you will naturally develop a burning desire to give them guidance and any social anxiety you could ever anticipate for all future events will fall away on their own accord.

> He who controls others may be powerful, but he who has
> mastered himself is mightier still.
> ~ Lao Tzu ~

On the next page, I am going to give you a golden key that will free you, from any *fear*, you may have, that will allow you to confidently communicate with a complete stranger or when speaking in front of a room full of people.

When I was 21 years old, I signed myself up for the renowned Dale Carnegie Course, knowing, in advance, that I would be required to public speak, in front of over forty of my peers, for the next 12 weeks. Not only was I the youngest person, attending, at the time, but my Instructor also informed me that I was the only student, who enrolled on own self-initiative and everyone else were registered, per employer requirements. I purposely decided to take this course, after I came across the statistics, stating that public speaking was amongst the top 3 things that people feared. As I previously mentioned, in the last chapter, *I insist on living life as fearlessly as possible.*

None of my classmates thought we would be expected to get up, in front of our group, on Orientation night, but I had a feeling that we would all be asked to at least introduce ourselves, so I prepared my speech in my car, while I was driving to the school. As soon as the instructor announced that we would all be required to stand up, in front of the classroom, and tell our classmates, something interesting about ourselves, you could physically *feel the fear* that filled the air after seeing everyone's frozen faces. As a teenager, I intuitively taught myself how to transform fear, into feelings of excitement and impulsively raised my right hand when they asked for a volunteer to go first. When I was speaking before my classmates, I could see that my confidence made many of them much calmer and by the end of Orientation, I was offered 3 opportunities for employment.

After the 1st official week of class, I quickly came to discover a secret that exploded my confidence throughout the remainder of the course and caused my classmates to honor me on graduation night with the prestigious Highest Award of Achievement. I am now turning the secret over to you and suggest you use it to your advantage at all times.

The most valuable lesson I learned while I was attending the Dale Carnegie course was that no one was concentrating on me when I was in front of the room. Their full focus was either on the speech they had just given or they were preparing themselves for their own approaching speech. I realized right away that there was no reason for me to ever feel insecure because I could clearly see that most of my classmates were **lost in their own little worlds**. The person who gets honored with the Highest Award of Achievement is based on the opinion of who each classmate as to who, displayed consistent confidence, throughout the entire course. The key reason why I won 42 out of 44 votes was because I truly was never nervous.

You can apply the same sound advice to any other social gathering you attend, by noticing that while you are carrying on a conversation with someone else, that other person's mind is racing, a mile a minute, trying to figure out what their response will be; subsequently, they are too preoccupied to pass judgment on you. You can always communicate, with confidence, when you remind yourself that everyone is more worried about what they will say than the words that are coming out of your mouth.

People may not remember exactly what you did, or what you said, but they will always remember how you made them feel.
~ Unknown ~

The media tends to put pressure on people to obsess over their looks, but the only way to leave a lasting impression on others is by being interested in *how you make them feel* and abandoning all past paranoia, about your appearance. It is important to attend to your looks, in whatever way is pleasing to you but you, never again need to worry if the right people will be attracted to you, based on your physical features. It is your personality that will pull in more business, friends and opportunities than you can handle. You will become addicted to all the attention you get when you make other people's feelings, more important, than impressing them.

113

I uncovered another little known fact about media advertising when I took several master marketing courses, back in 2005, and it aggravates me, to this day, every time I come across a commercial or website that incorporates the treacherous technique, I am about to share with you. The common theme, in many of my marketing books, suggests instilling fear in the minds of potential customers. "Act now because this offer may not be available by tomorrow", "If you don't take advantage of the opportunity today, then things could get progressively worse" and the latest craze for commercials is "In this bad economy" etc.

No wonder why, most of the world is walking around, anxious, all the time. We are constantly being blasted with strong messages of doom and gloom, every time, we turn on the television or open up a newspaper. It is no secret that these marketing companies are experts when it comes to The Pain and Pleasure Principle but the working world does not have the time to study such subjects. The Pain and Pleasure Principle is proven to be the governing guide to virtually every action we engage or avoid. Simply put, the principle states that people are driven to take actions that gain pleasure or avoid pain. You would think that most people would be motivated to take actions that deliver desirable results but research, reports that most people are prone to avoid pain, over seeking pleasure. Similar to the Fight or Flight Response System, most people never realize that there is always a 3rd, 4th and 5th option to choose from. What about Fight, Flight or Alright? Why are we taught that our only two options are to put up a fight or run away, like a coward, when we also have the option of creating crowd pleasing outcomes?

"The Pebble Story", by Edward De Bono, that I am about to share with you will open your mind even more, and prove to you that there is always a way to get what you want when you ponder other options, outside of the obvious:

Many years ago, when a debtor could be thrown into jail, a merchant in London had the misfortune to owe a huge sum to a moneylender. The moneylender, who was old and ugly, fancied the merchant's beautiful teenaged daughter. He proposed a bargain. He said that he would cancel the merchant's debt if he could have the girl.

Both the merchant and his daughter were horrified at the proposal. So the cunning moneylender proposed that they let providence decide the matter. He told them that he would put a black pebble and a white pebble into an empty money bag and then the girl would pick out one of the pebbles. If she chose the black pebble, she would become his wife and her father's debt would be canceled. If she chose the white pebble, she would stay with her father and the debt still would be canceled. But if she refused to pick out the pebble, her father would be thrown into jail and she would starve.

Reluctantly, the merchant agreed. They were standing on a pebble-strewn path in the merchant's garden as they talked, and the money-lender stooped down to pick up the two pebbles. As he picked up the pebbles, the girl, sharp-eyed with fright, notice that he picked up two black pebbles and put them into the money bag. He then told the girl to pick out the pebble that was to decide her fate and that of her father.

Instructions: Picture your self as the girl in the story.

1. How would you have handled the situation?
2. If you had to advise her, what would you advise her to do?
3. How did you reach your solution (briefly explain your thinking)?

After analyzing "The Pebble Story," vertical thinkers would arrive at three possible solutions:

1. The girl should refuse to take a pebble.
2. The girl should show that there are two black pebbles in the bag and expose the moneylender as a cheat.
3. The girl should take a black pebble and sacrifice herself in order to save her father from prison.

However, none of these suggestions is very helpful. If the girl does not take a pebble, her father will go to prison; if she does take a pebble, she will be forced to marry the moneylender.

In contrast to vertical thinkers who are concerned with the fact that the girl has to take a pebble, lateral thinkers focus on the pebble that is left behind. Vertical thinkers take the most reasonable view of a situation and then proceed logically and carefully to work it out. Lateral thinkers tend to explore all the different ways of looking at something, rather than accepting the most promising view and proceeding from that. Therefore, lateral thinkers would be more likely to find this solution to the problem:

The girl in the "Pebble Story" put her hand into the money bag and drew out a pebble. Without looking at it, she fumbled and let it fall to the path, where it immediately was lost amongst all the other pebbles. "Oh, how clumsy of me," she said, "But never mind, if you look into the bag, you will be able to tell which pebble I took by the color of the one that is left."

Because the remaining pebble was, of course, black, it must be assumed that she had taken out the white pebble – the moneylender dared not admit his honesty. By using lateral thinking, the girl changed what seemed to be an impossible situation into an extremely advantageous one. The girl actually was better off now than if the moneylender had been honest and had put one black and one white pebble into the bag, for then she would have had only a 50 percent chance of being saved. As it happened, she was sure of remaining with her father and, at the same time, of having his debt canceled.

From: NEW THINK: THE USE OF LATERAL THINKING IN THE GENERATION OF NEW IDEAS by EDWARD DE BONO. **Reprinted by permission of BASIC BOOKS, a member of Perseus Books Group.**

Another important point we can conclude from the story of the merchant and his daughter is that not everyone, we interact with, will be good natured or nice. We were all told when we were little, "If you don't have anything nice to say, then don't say anything at all" and the goal has always been to be a good person. Our conditioning has caused us to give people the benefit of the doubt, even those that do not deserve it, and stops us from "calling a spade a spade". The reality, however, is that *there are people who will talk badly behind your back, and* ruin your reputation for their own selfish reasons, even though you befriended them. Stop trying to find the good in these people. Be wise enough to outsmart anyone, who would deliberately deceive you. **It does not make you a "good person" to let other people take advantage of you but it will make you a well respected role model when you stay one step ahead of your adversaries.**

It is painstakingly clear that what all people want and are in desperate need of is…INSPIRATION. Intimidation techniques fail for everyone involved, in the long run, and instant gratification leaves people feeling emptier than before, but inspiration has the power to permanently transform a person, while it provides a platform for catapulting quantum leaps in life.

Now that the blinders are off, you can see straight through the scare tactics and stop yourself from spreading the fear around, when conversing with others. Prepare yourself for the next time that someone you work with or care about makes a comment that confesses their fear; rather than automatically agreeing or sympathizing with them, offer something inspiration to them. In doing this, get ready for all the gratitude you'll receive, for *you have given them hope*, unlike everyone else, who makes them feel that there is no way out of their misery. Inspiration is the reason why Rocky Balboa movies have been steady best sellers since the 1970's. Inspiration is also the reason that Oprah Winfrey was able to rise up from poverty to billionaire level, because she willingly dedicated her entire life, to being an inspiration to as many people as possible.

Those who play on other people's fear, for fast cash, should not be surprised when the Universe sends them a hardship that depletes them of their funds, just as fast. But the person, who takes the road less traveled and insists on inspiring others, will be blessed beyond belief. It would be equally easy for marketers, rather than employ fear-based antics to secure their potential buyer, to instead, offer incentives and power-packed inspirations. By making this one minor modification, they could quickly quadruple their profit line.

You do not have to build a business around inspiring other people or go out of your way to boost anybody's confidence, but it will benefit you tremendously, to avoid any interactions that revolve around fear and always do your best to see the silver lining in the sky, when speaking with others.

If you realized how powerful your thoughts are, you would never think a negative thought.
~ Peace Pilgrim (1908-1981) ~

Underneath the layer of lies, which have been heaped on you your whole life, there remains a paradisiacal part of your being that is perfect. You are none of the bad names, you may have been called, and when you cast out all the negative thoughts, you have believed about yourself, you will never again look at life or other people, in the same light.

Just as no two snowflakes are alike, YOU are a one-of-a-kind. *There never was and never will be another human being who will embody your exact body, brain, custom code, finger prints, gifts, soul, talents and thoughts.* You can consult one of the millions of scientific books available that will confirm the dozens of different components that make you unlike anyone else. We slam the door shut on all of our dreams when we waste our time, comparing ourselves to other people. Do not spend another minute, wishing you were anything like anyone else, because you were born to be an original.

If you love singing, but it is not one of your strengths, then sing for fun and find out what you were destined to do. I have known, since I was in sixth grade, that I would be a writer when I grew up, but I always had this thought in the back of my mind that maybe...just maybe...there was something even more exciting that I could be doing. I spent several years of my life, looking for any far-fetched opportunity that would be "way cooler", than a writing career, but all I did was set myself back, big time. I finally snapped out of my foolishness and wrote my first book, when I was 26 years old. I now have 5 books under my belt and I could write another book all about how much I love writing for a living!!!

When you do what you love, the money **WILL** follow. *Don't let anyone talk you out of doing what you love and stop telling yourself that you are not good enough.* My average grade in English was a C- and time after time, all I ever heard were people, telling me there was no way I would make it as an author. In spite of this, I refused to let anyone talk me out of believing in myself, and look at who got the last laugh!!!

There is greatness, living inside of you and the sooner you peel away all the lies that have been covering up **YOUR** uniqueness, then that is when your life will start running smoother than a well oiled machine.

In the next Chapter we will start to take inventory of all the things that you are passionate about, but first, we must make room, in your mind, for the clues to come through, clearly.

Before falling off to sleep tonight, bring to mind, any negative names you have been silently saying to yourself such as "I am not good enough", "I am not smart enough", "I am far from perfect" and anything else that goes against the greatness, you were born with. Think back to when you were a baby and recall that there was a time, when your mind did not contain negative thoughts, about yourself or the world around you. You were born with the innocence to believe in yourself, for all the days of your life. In all reality, any bad mouthing being done by you, or being said about you by another, is an outright lie. Are you willing to live with these lies, when you were born to be great?

I couldn't believe how many horrible labels I had lodged in my subconscious mind, when I took the time to tune into them. I immediately cast out every thought that thwarted the greatness, buried within my being, despite some bad habits, I still had. This single action, alone, slung shot my success. Imagine *how fast* **you** can move forward, in the direction of your dearest dreams, when you aren't weighed down by destructive thoughts.

Bad habits, addictions and attitudes stem entirely from the countless deceptions that we were conditioned into believing, about ourselves. When we release the lies, that cast shadows on the truth, i.e. that **greatness lives within us**; the negative vices will vanish on their own.

Say the following statement, out loud and proud...

I, (your name), do solemnly swear, to stop saying negative things about myself and I will do my very best to never again buy into or believe anything that goes against the greatness that exists inside my being. I make the definite decision to be the *best me*, that I can be, and I will work with what I already have, to custom create every earthly experience that will give me great joy!!!

Procuring Your Passions and Wildest Wishes

Above all, be true to yourself, and if you can not put your heart
into, take yourself out of it.
~ Hardy D. Jackson ~

What feelings would you experience, if I placed a picture of
a lion, in front of your face? If you are not a lion lover, like I am,
then chances are you wouldn't feel much of anything, right? Now,
imagine what it would feel like if a lion was on the loose and
standing 10 feet away from you. Picturing the life you love, and
physically living the life you love, are as different as night and day.
You may have spent most of your life, lost in thought about your
picture perfect world, but the instant you learn how to live from
your heart and not your head, your wildest wishes will become
waking reality.

Handing "matters of the heart", over to the head, is as pre-
posterous as breaking a full length mirror, in hopes of changing our
figure. We can quickly move from frustration, to fulfillment, when
we take control over our mechanical minds and awaken in the
moment to where our heart has all the answers. *Here's a hint...*start
searching your heart for the answers and after they arrive, then
apply your mind power into making them manifest. We are "driving in reverse" when we rack our brains for answers that it does not
have and end up even further away from where we want to go.

Most people have appointed their head as the CEO, over
their life, *but the proper position of the mind was always meant to be the
personal assistant to the human heart* and to make sure that all requests
are executed to the exciting end result that is expected. Your heart
possesses the passion, that your head has been forever, searching
for, and we will get yours pumping like a powerful water well.

If someone you trusted warned you in advance that you were about to walk into a hidden hole that dropped down five miles below ground level and no man made equipment could pull you out, would you continue in the direction you were "headed" or turn around at once? The mistake that mankind has been making, since the beginning of time, has been in trusting the head and never knowing that the heart contains everything we have been looking for, our whole life. The mind can not help but run rampant, like a wild horse, until its master steps on the scene and takes charge over the beautiful beast.

Your mind is not the friend you may believe it to be. It has been trained to act against you, as you will soon see, but that all stops today. *You can gain control over your mind, in a matter of minutes, and make it pull in all of your passions, by simply resetting it, the right way.* Right now, we will reset your mind such that it no longer resists the material, you are mastering, then we will move on to procuring your personal passions and wildest wishes, at the end of this of this chapter.

The mind, that most people put all their trust into, is presently programmed to run on autopilot and operates much like a machine, that spits outs useless thoughts, every millisecond. Have you not noticed that 9 out of 10 of these random thoughts, that cross our mind every minute, are more hurtful than anything, another human being has ever said to us? From the minute we open our eyes, in the morning, until the second we fall asleep at night, our mind is rambling all day long, about what failures we are, and how we will never amount to anything.

You can lie to me and everyone else that these thoughts don't run through your mind, on a daily basis, but you can not lie to yourself. We have ALL been through this internal torment, since the beginning of man's existence. Regrettably, to this day, most people have never learned how to escape this hellish existence because they spend their entire life, trying to fight off these enemy thoughts or even worse, learn to live with them. Fortunately, however, it just so happens that we can cruise *control* "on easy street", wherein, bypassing these thoughts all together...

A double minded man is unstable in all his ways.
~ James 1:8 (K.J.V.) ~

The same way a DVD player can only project one movie on the screen, at a time, your mind can only think one thought at a time. The double minded man argues, all day long, with the cynical thoughts that his mechanical mind spits out, by fighting back with defensive thoughts. After fighting back for hours, day in and day out, the double minded man begins to grow weary and gives into these thoughts, by believing them.

The mechanical mind: "You are never going to be rich".

The double minded man: "There has got to be a way for me to make more money".

The mechanical mind: "Even if there was a way...you're not smart enough to succeed".

The double minded man: "I am too, smart enough, and I could always go back to school if I needed to".

The mechanical mind: "You don't have time to go to school and even if you only attended part-time, how the hell are you going to pay for it".

The double minded man: "Maybe I can start a business instead of going back to school".

The mechanical mind: "You don't know the first thing about operating your own business".

The double minded man: "I know, looks like I am stuck where I am for now but maybe one day I will find a way to feel fulfilled".

The example, above, is only one of literally hundreds of conversations, taking place between the mechanical mind and the double minded man, every single day. And while I hate to be the bearer of bad news, in reality, the double minded man represents nearly everyone. Note that I said, "nearly", thereby indicative of the slight majority of people, fortunate enough to have escaped this double-minded mentality. Nevertheless, these thoughts do not vanish into thin air, as much as we wish they did, but instead, they enter into the esoteric universe where the mechanical mind is permanently tuned into, like a radio station. Unlike the mechanical mind, the heart is permanently tuned into infinite intelligence, where we can receive all of the answers we desire, when we are tuned into the right station. The heart resides in the present moment and we can access the information we want when we are attentive, to the "now".

YOU HAVE NEVER KNOWN HOW BECAUSE YOU HAVE NEVER KNOWN...NOW!!!

The double minded man thinks that the thoughts being broadcasted from the mechanical mind are coming from him/her own self, never discovering the true source or simple solution, to tune out this madness. Although invisible, the collective thoughts of mass consciousness are moving through the air, at all times, the same way that waveforms constantly communicate with your entertainment and electrical devices. *It is within your power to turn off that annoying, mechanical mind "set"*, just as easily as you would turn off a television program or radio station that was airing anything of an annoying nature.

If you chase two rabbits, both will escape.
~ Chinese Proverb ~

The reason why most people find it impossible to achieve any level of success, outside of the ordinary, is because they have no idea how to ignore the mechanical mind, thus, being unable to intentionally direct their individual thought power. Your thoughts are very powerful forces **when** they are *not* coming from the mechanical mind *and* **only** **when** intentions are set into motion, from firm decisions that *YOU* consciously choose. Bouncing back and forth from bad thoughts to good thoughts, throughout the day, is as frivolous as chasing two rabbits because you will always end up empty handed. Until you insist on silencing the mechanical mind, it would be a waste of time to pull your passions out of subconscious storage, because the interference will continue to distract you from your dreams and desires, as it has always done.

Your mind would have you believe that it takes years to heal from hardships and gain complete control over your life. The wisdom, within your heart, knows that transformation started the second you desired it to, and that any time lapsed, is due to all the doubt that is invading the mind. Are you ready to turn your back on the mind that has been antagonizing you, and without any further delay, tune into the heart that has all of your answers?

You can take charge over your mind, as quickly as a trained lion tamer gains control over the king of the jungle, by mastering the moment at hand. As comforting as it has been to abandon the present moment, by relishing in memories from the past, and day dreaming about all the things that could come our way in the future, this mechanical mind thought pattern will immobilize your personal power. The head is accustomed to being in charge, as it thrives on the laziness of living in the obsolete past and fictitious future. However, the heart can tap into the true power that achieves the impossible, with a lot less effort than the exhausting games that the mechanical mind likes to play.

Trust no future, however pleasant! Let the dead past bury its
dead! Act – act in the living present! Heart within and Go
overhead.
~ Henry Wadsworth Longfellow (1807-1882) ~

The *"living present"* is the only, point in time, where true
power will ever exist and can supply you with an endless stream of
energy that makes manifesting your desires seem effortless.

Thinking about the past and the future is like looking at pic-
tures, in a magazine, of all the things you love. The present moment provides you, with the power to take action, today, on your
personal passions and will place you in possession of all the things
that make life, worth living!!!

The floodgates of fortune will fly open, faster then you can
count to ten, when you stop trusting your mind and dismissing your
heart. If…starting today, you make the bold decision to trust your
heart and make your mind attend to the present moment, then, you
will find, in less than one month, your life to be better than it has
ever been.

Knowing that nothing can get in our way, other than our own
mind, **what do you think** is the easiest way to tackle the trickery?

a) Argue with these thoughts all day long
b) Give into these thoughts and abandon your dreams
c) Turn the tables on these thoughts by outsmarting them
d) Let these thoughts pass by like clouds without clinging to
them and return your attention to the present moment

The clear-cut answer comes from the famous expression,
"Get your head out of the clouds". Realize right now, and for all
time, that there is nothing to be gained, by getting lost in thought.

Everything you could ever desire exists right now!!! When your awareness is on high alert, to the magnetic power of the present moment, you start the cycle of pulling in, all of the things you've been placing your attention on. Awaken at once, to the power that, at this very moment, is permeating the space that surrounds you, and then, intentionally **tap into it today**, for rapid results.

In chapter 2, we went over one of life's little secret, which was, "The projector is responsible for the picture that appears on the screen. YOU are the projector. The world is the screen. *You have the power and permission to change the reality being reflected, in any instant, if you so desire.* If images of lack and struggle are all over the screen, simply insert the disc, with all the images of the wealth you want".

If you had your heart set on renting a romantic comedy, would you let the sales associate at the video store, talk you into renting a murder-mystery movie instead? I highly doubt it. Why then, would you let your mind, talk you out of your dreams and desires? *Mastering your mind* and making it project your picture perfect world, on the outside screen called "life", can be as effortless as exchanging discs in a DVD player. Is your mind telling you right now, that there is no way you can make changes in life, this easy? Also, are you willing to continue to believe these thoughts, when you have the choice to choose, thoughts that can quickly bring about *exciting and extraordinary change?*

At any instant, **you** can interrupt the movie that your mind has been playing on repeat and intentionally insert all of the images you would like to be played out, in your life. You can plug the projector into the power source that will bring your picture to life by awakening your entire being, in the present moment.

Have you ever been caught in the middle of a conversation, with two people that are trying to talk over each, vying for your attention? One of these people is saying something of significance and the other person is saying something that is utterly useless. You do your best, to tune into both of them, by looking back and forth, between the two talkers, but become drained, rather fast, from this pin-pong and realize that nothing that either of them said, has sunk in. You are then put in the position, to ask one over the other, to start back at the beginning and repeat what they were saying.

Your heart is speaking to you, every single millisecond and at the same time that your mind is throwing random thoughts at you. That still and small voice, from within, is your heart, speaking to you, in the form of *feelings*. Those persons, who unknowingly allow, their mind to run on autopilot and spend most of their moments, lost in thought, are pulled away from their feelings. The reason why most people are afraid of their feelings is because they "hang out" inside their heads, out of sheer habit. We've already acknowledged that 9 out of every 10 of the random thoughts that run through our head are harmful and hurtful. All of the fear, that we are feeling, is coming from the head and yet, *that is where we escape to, when we attempt to avoid pain???*

The heart does not know fear nor does it recognize feelings of a negative nature. The heart is the store house for all passionate, positive and powerful feelings. *We all have the power, to turn a hellish existence into a heavenly experience, by choosing to listen to our heart, instead of living in our head.*

Here is how easy it is to "tune into our heart" and enter into enduring happiness…

If it *feels* good and makes your spirit sing…go for it!!!
If it *feels* wrong and drags you down…steer clear at all costs!!!

Rumor has it that we may only come around this way once. If your heart says, "I am not happy here" and your head answers back, "I am afraid to make changes", who are you going to let guide you, from now on? It is time to gradually begin, replacing the people, places and things in your life that make you feel bad or blah, and simultaneously include more of the things that fill you with feelings of freedom and happiness.

Ironically, before I began writing this chapter, this morning, I received an e-mail, from the creator of "Quantum Jumping", Burt Goldman, who is 81 years old. I couldn't resist clicking on his link that allowed me to access his website, after reading his brief biography. Burt Goldman began tapping into his passion after he entered the senior citizen stage. Just before turning 80, Burt, took up painting and now, he has his artwork, proudly displayed in a public museum.

This amazing man also authored multiple novels, started a million-dollar online business and had many of the photographs that he took, accepted into the International Photography Hall of Fame, at the age where most people have, long since, relaxed into retirement.

If Burt Goldman can create a million-dollar online business after becoming a senior citizen, then whatever age you are, right now, is ideal for you to start producing one passion, after the other. *I can't emphasize it enough...* **You can** accomplish as much or more, than Burt did, if you'd like, by <u>mastering your mechanical mind **and** consciously creating the desires of your heart.</u>

Are you ready to lay it, *all on the line*, and *take the leap of faith* that ushers you from *"imaging to inventing"*?

And said, Verily I say unto you, Except ye be converted, and become as little children, ye shall not enter into the kingdom of heaven.
~ Matthew 18:3 (K.J.V.) ~

The mechanical mind has been weighing us down with difficult and heavy thoughts, having hardened us into the serious adults that we are today. The second we stop engaging in defensive dialogs, with all these random thoughts, and start inserting specific instructions, the thousands of daunting thoughts will not only die down but *we will experience, firsthand, how empowering it feels, to master one's own mind.* Those persons, who have mastered their own minds, look at life like their personal playground and have walked away from the world where everything is taken so seriously.

You can not enter into the kingdom of creation until you convert from being a serious adult, into an adventurous child. There is a very vast difference between being childish, and being childlike. You are not being instructed to act immature or throw temper tantrums to get what you want, as are the actions of a toddler, **but** *you are expected to approach manifesting with a happy heart and have fun while you are consciously creating.* Little children are not taught how to tap into the power of intention, when they are playing with their imaginations, and that is precisely why, when we grow into adulthood, we do not believe that *our concentrated thoughts are the key to creating.* And inasmuch as most adults are aware of the power of intention, they are, instead, encouraged to exert great physical force, with an itty-biddy amount of imagination. So, now you can see why most people end up accomplishing very little, over a long period of time.

You will begin to manifest more dreams, in one month, than most people do, in a year, *when you master the science of mixing the perfect amount of imagination with the perfect amount of intention.*

My earliest recollection of mixing "imagination", with "intention", dates back to when I was thirteen years old. I am going to share with you, my true story, "Two Front Teeth", to better explain, blending "imagination", with, "intention" and *then we will effortlessly pour out* **your passions**, *on paper.*

I started to become self-conscious about my two, crooked front teeth, the year I officially became a teenager. While the rest of my teeth were fairly straight, my two front teeth overlapped one another. After a few weeks of obsessing over my criss-cross smile, I decided that I was going to ask my dad about getting braces. I hated the thought of having metal in my mouth, for a minimum of two years, but I would be willing to do that if it meant having a perfect smile, for the rest of my life.

Before I approached my dad, I was completely clear about wanting straight teeth and my certainty established a *knowing*, from within, that I would get what I wanted, without any worry about "how" or "when". I *intended* to get my straight smile and <u>never attached to the idea that my dad was the **only way**</u> I could get what I wanted, therefore, nothing on the outside disrupted my inner *knowing*. I didn't know *when* or *how*, I was going to acquire my chic smile but I certainly knew that I wanted it now!!! The thought that I would have to wait never entered my mind.

I didn't feel the need to have a sit-down discussion with my dad, about getting braces, so, I spontaneously stopped him while he was walking by and nonchalantly asked, "Does your dental insurance cover braces"? My dad's response was, "I'm not sure but I will find out this week when I am at work". I was happy with his answer and went back to watching television.

I gave my dad a full week to find out, from his Human Resource Department, if his insurance covered the cost of braces, before I approached him again. All week long, while I was waiting on my dad, I *imagined* in my mind; looking into a mirror and seeing myself as already having a sparkling, straight smile. As I sat down next to my dad, while he was flipping through one of his Golf Magazines, I asked him if he found out about whether or not his insurance plan, included braces. My dad informed me that since braces were considered cosmetic, his particular plan did not cover them, adding that he did not have the two thousand dollars, to pay the "out of pocket" expenses. Feeling bad about not being able to afford my braces, at this time, my dad said, "I will try to save some money, each month, and hopefully I might be able to get you braces next year". I put my hand on his arm and said, "Don't worry Dad…I *know* everything will work out!!!"

That weekend, a group of us decided to go sleigh-riding, on the side streets. The snow plows had pushed the piled-up snow, off to the side of the street, creating a slide-like setting. My friend, Michelle, asked me if I wanted to try sleighing down, on the side of the street, instead of the street itself. It sounded like fun to me, so I agreed to go down with her, but only if I could sit in the front. The snow bank, we were sliding down, was much slicker than the snow on the street, as it didn't have a hard surface, to slow down our speed. Halfway down the hill, my friend became afraid of how much speed we were gaining, and she grabbed onto a telephone pole, in an attempt to stop the sleigh. The impact, of this impulsive maneuver, spun the sled around, and my face slammed into the telephone pole.

I could barely feel my fingers because it was so cold, and that could be the reason why my face did not hurt, after crashing into the telephone pole. I asked my friend, Michelle, if she was alright, but she was in bad shape and said that it felt like she pulled her arm, out of its socket. The rest of our group came running to our aid. One of them pointed out to me that my mouth was bleeding. I glided my glove, across my lower lip, confirming that I was bleeding, but thankfully, my mouth did not hurt. After the accident, we all packed up our sleighs and decided to "call it a night".

As I walked through my front door, my mom started screaming for my dad, because she saw the blood on my face and could see from across the kitchen, that my two front teeth were severely chipped. I ran into the bathroom, to see for myself, just how badly chipped, my two front teeth were. I looked like a hockey player, who just got hit in the mouth, by a fast-flying puck. My dad immediately put my mind at ease, by reassuring me that he would rush me to the dentist, first thing, in the morning.

My dad awakened, before me, scheduling an emergency appointment for me to see my dentist, later that morning. Once I did wake up, I felt fortunate that my mouth still wasn't experiencing any soreness. But more then that, I was extremely excited, over the prospect of seeing my dentist that day, because I knew he was going to repair my two front teeth, making them as straight as the rest of my other teeth. Later that day, my dentist molded two temporary caps, thereby catapulting my self-confidence, and one week later, I was "out and about", proudly displaying my perfectly straight pair of permanent porcelain caps.

By taking this story into account, in conjunction with all my other manifestation stories, previously mentioned, *can you see just how fast my desires manifested into physical reality?*

I not only acquired my desirable, straight smile, within two weeks, but I also avoided the need to wear braces for two years! However, *the best part of this experience was* that while both caps cost the same as the cost of braces, my dad's dental insurance covered the complete cost of the procedure because it was considered emergency, and not cosmetic. I know that having your teeth knocked out doesn't sound like a pleasant path, towards getting a straight smile, and I would be the first one, to agree with you, *if* I had experienced any degree of pain or could not get to the dentist the next day. However, I did not suffer any pain, in the slightest. I will admit and share with you that I thoroughly enjoyed the entire process because *I felt completely astounded, attributable to my own personal involvement, with the anticipation and unfolding of my desire.*

If a teenager and a senior citizen can quickly manifest their desires, then there is no reason why you can not do the same, starting today!!!

Now it's your turn to take over the spotlight!!! Let's set all seriousness aside, and get into the spirit of "playing pretend". The power of intention is not necessary, right now, and will be initiated in chapter 15. However, before we begin, you will need your notebook and a pen, because we will be organizing your answers, in another chapter.

Your *head* would have this exercise be hard, silly and strenuous but your *heart* will have your passions, pouring out faster than you can write them down. For the time being, please put perfectionism on the back burner and allow your imagination to whisk you away, like a little child lost in play, as you work through the following exciting exercise…

Unbeknownst to you, your cousin entered your information, into a contest, wanting you to be completely surprised, if you ended up being the winner. Now, imagine receiving word that you are the winner of this whimsical contest. You find out from the caller that the prize you won is one full day, with a fairy godmother, ready to grant you your every wish, including any wishes that encompass the rest of your life.

You have eight straight hours to write out your wish list, in the presence of your fairy god mother. She will then help you determine if the desires, you list, are from your head or from your heart and she will not depart, until you both feel great about the finalized draft. Then, once your time together is done, she will see to it that everything you've specified will come to pass. Now that the stage has been set, all you are expected to do, right now, is to write out your **rough draft**, and allow all of you wildest wishes to go from "think" to "ink".

Just a friendly reminder…Your *head* would have this exercise be hard, silly and strenuous but your *heart* will have your passions, pouring out faster than you can write them down. Let your imagination make this experience *feel* real and set aside all seriousness as you work through the exciting exercise above.

The clock is ticking and the task at hand is much too important, to lose track of time…so, **start writing** *before your 8-hour window of opportunity closes!!!*

Calling Forth Your Exclusive Core Craving

To be yourself in a world that is constantly trying to make you something else is the greatest accomplishment.
~ Ralph Waldo Emerson (1803-1882) ~

Most people spend their whole life searching for their true purpose or don't believe that there is something special that they are destined to do. Some people are aware of what their purpose is but are unsure of how to cross the threshold and breakthrough, to their perfect path. There are also those people, who are passionately pursuing their purpose and could always use positive reinforcement or that extra push, during periods of plateau. All of the above will be addressed, throughout this chapter.

No amount of money can ever compare to the thrill and security that springs forth from discovering your exclusive core craving. Many people would rather win the lottery instead of discovering their reason for being born, but research analysis reports that one third of all multimillion dollar winners end up filing for bankruptcy, after a few years of winning the gigantic jackpot. Unlike the lottery, cracking the code to your exclusive core craving is completely within your control and warrants happiness that will last a lifetime.

We were all born to be wildly wealthy and our one guaranteed way, to getting there, lies in discovering our life's purpose. If we are having a hard time, managing $45K a year, how can we trust ourselves to manage many times that amount? *By aligning our life, love and work with our most desirable destiny, we can handle anything that comes our way, especially abundance.*

Any anxiety and fear you feel, comes from not knowing, forgetting or failing to take action on fulfilling your true purpose!!!

There is nothing wrong with leading a life of comfort but there is also no harm in figuring out, once and for all, the singular area where you could contribute better than anyone else alive. Life is a lot like one big puzzle and your individuality is one of the necessary pieces that it takes to complete the picture. We have all experienced how puzzling life can be and without YOU, the picture would be incomplete. *Like every puzzle piece, you most definitely do have a designated spot where you fit in perfectly and when you discover your true purpose, you will feel wholeness that can not be described with words, even if you aren't yet ready to situate into your spot.*

This chapter will give you greater clarity as to the true definition of a person's purpose and melt away any mental blocks that have been keeping you from realizing your own. Also note that we will be calculating your financial freedom figure, throughout Chapter 15, which we will plug it into the "Strive for Five" system, to start the process of prospering. Go grab your notebook and get ready to do some jaw-dropping discovering!!!

Most people are under the misconception that discovering their purpose is a tedious task of leaving no stone unturned, devouring every career book that they come across, or endlessly sitting in silence, for an answer to appear. The truth is, your life purpose is so much more than your occupation and you have already received various signs, along the way, as to what it is. What you do and who you are destined to be is like comparing apples to oranges. I may presently be an author but my true purpose in life is to create extraordinary moments, out of ordinary experiences and transform as many lives as possible, along the way. I do this in my daily life, outside of publishing and I get asked, all the time, "Are you always this happy"? I tell every inquirer, how much I truly love the life I live and then slip them my business card with my website address, for additional information.

Choose a job you love, and you will never have to work a day in your life.
~ Confucius (551-479 BCE) ~

Life has been giving you all of your clues, since you were a small child, as to what you are destined to do, but at the same time, society has been preparing you and training you, for the work force. When you *choose* a job that you love, instead of striving for a high paying position that promises the stars and the sun, work will feel like play and an abundance of money will avalanche into your world. *The only real job security in this world is an undying devotion to one's true purpose.* Since experience speaks louder than words, would you be willing to take the simple steps that map out your perfect path and places you on the Amtrak to total fulfillment? GREAT…then you *ARE* ready to get going!!!

I've implemented the following tools and techniques, to bring to bear, my true purpose, in less time than it takes to watch a "Lord of the Rings" movie. These series of questions and suggestions will eradicate all stigmas that imply discovering your true purpose has to be hard. It is time to tune out the outside world and stop allowing society to push you down a path that you have no desire to travel. Start seeing to it that the strongest voice AND the *only voice*, in your life, is the one that is coming from within **YOU**.

It is time to take the "Pick Only One" self-discovery survey…

1. If you could only talk about one topic for the rest of your life, what would it be?

2. What hours of the day do you desire to work?

3. What is your ideal work environment?

4. What type of lifestyle would you love to lead?

5. What is your favorite form of communication?

6. What do other people most often praise you for or pay you compliments on?

7. What is the one area that you outshine everyone else in your social circle?

8. What are you naturally good at, that others are not?

9. What activities do you love so much that you lose track of time and could talk about with others, for hours?

10. What desirable line of work flashes through your mind, every month, but you are afraid to explore it further?

11. What would make you happier than you have ever been?

12. How much money do you need to make, every month, to cover your current expenses?

13. If you could locate or create the perfect position that was tailored around all of your answers above, _would you_ take the plunge, _if you knew_ there were no way you could fail?

14. **Will you**, _start seeking out this opportunity_, **today**?

All of your affinities and passions point you to your true purpose. _Unfortunately, most people are not leading lives that involve or revolve around their purpose, because they are out of sync with their inner voice._ They've been taught to trust the outside world, over their individual intuition. Then again, there are times, when the answers seem all too easy and obvious, that we shove them aside due to disbelief or they "fly right over our heads", altogether.

In a minute, I am going to share with you, how my good friend, Christina, finally discovered *her* purpose, this past year, and how the answer was staring us both, square in the face, for years. Her belief that "the hunt had to be harder than the awesome answers that she already received", kept her off of her passionate path, much longer than she would have liked.

My friend Christina enjoys teaching Earth Science to high school students but she wakes up, each day, with an intense feeling, from within, that she is destined to do more. We have been in each other's lives, for over 4 years now, and try to make an effort to meet up, at least once a week, to exchange manifestation stories. For as long as I have known Christina, she is as committed as anyone could be, in attempting to uncover their own *personally-tailored purpose*, and I have been by her side, while she experimented with various vocational ventures.

Throughout the years, I have made several suggestions to Christina as to what I could see her doing that would make a major difference in people's lives and create ever lasting success for herself. However, in the final analysis, my friend's destiny is for her, and her alone, to discover.

One afternoon, while we were having lunch at Applebee's, Christina was not as upbeat as usually and vented to me that she was about to abandon her dreams of discovering her destiny. I could see that my friend was in no mood to focus, but still, I immediately started to ask her the same 14 questions that I shared with you, while I committed to paying very close attention to her answers. By the time the waiter brought us our bill, my friend and I were able to narrow in on her core exclusive craving.

My friend is fascinated with anything and everything, having to do with angels. There was a time in my life, when I was not a big believer in angels and Christina talked me into attending an angel's course, with her, hoping to open my mind, about them. I have since become a believer though I still don't think about them nearly as often as she does. Christina has given me several angel figurines as gifts and I have been buying her an assortment of angel-themed items, throughout the years. We also find ourselves talking about angels, for hours, when we're together and coincidentally, my nickname for her has always been "earth angel". *How did we not discover this sooner???*

After taking into account, all of her other answers to the "Pick Only One" self-discovery survey, we were able to put together the perfect plan for my friend to fulfill her passion and purpose. Since then, my friend has never been happier and she has finally satisfied that feeling, from within. When we do what we are meant to do, rather than work for money, the wealth will follow and start to flow freely like never before. Wealth is sought by many but found by few because the last place that most people would ever think to look to is at their passions and purpose for prosperity.

Take a long hard look at your life and pay attention to all of the things that you love. What is that one activity or area that you always think to yourself," I can do this better than them" or "I would love to make a living out of this, like they do"?

My passion for writing this particular book has been brewing in the back of my mind for years. The four previous books, I've written, have nothing to do with manifesting, but they were all topics that I was most passionate about, at the time, and I have been actively writing, all along. The true purpose for writing this particular book is because *this is the book that I always wanted to read!!!*

I spent years, searching for a book, about manifesting, that cut-out the technical mumbo-jumbo and would provide me multiple examples from one person, who repeatedly applied the formula, as opposed to isolated incidents, experienced by several different people. I never understood why most of the books, based on manifesting more money, would tip-toe around the topic at hand. I also wanted to be made aware of any possible obstacles that could come up and be provided with swift and straightforward solutions. Last but not least, I sought reassurance, throughout every chapter, that I have what it takes to succeed because, if I don't believe in myself, then no system will work.

Without fail, it seemed that every time I finished reading one of the countless books, that I disappointedly devoted so much time into, I would always end up thinking to myself, "Maybe the next book I find will "*be the one*". Of course, the desire for *me* to "be the one" to write the book always came to mind too, but I was busy, pursuing other passions. I arrived at the definite decision to create this book, in the exact manner I've envisioned it should be, after having received requests, from an overwhelming number of people, asking me to explain the steps that I apply, in manifesting my good fortune. All of the pieces fell into place for me to write this book and I will not be distraught if I don't sell a single copy because my true purpose will have already been fulfilled. When you are taking all action from a place of **true purpose**, you will naturally *know* what it means to desire without any attachment, as is required per, "The Unspoken Formula to Fast Fortunes".

Everything you want is out there waiting for you to ask. Everything you want also wants you. But you have to take action to get it.
~ Jules Renard (1846-1910) ~

The most powerful point to take from the quote above is that "*Everything you want also wants you*". It dawned on me, one day, that *if I desired for all of those years, to write a comprehensive book about manifesting, then droves of other people must possess the desire to read those writings.* Throughout the years, while I devoted my time and energy into pursuing other passions, my desire to write about manifestation never diminished. On the contrary, that particular desire actually intensified, with each passing year.

The desires of your heart come from your higher self, in hopes of satisfying the "supply and demand" desires that will serve that specific multitude. *Are you starting to see how important it is that you pursue your passions and purpose?* "Everything you want also wants you" and the desires of your heart, made manifest, will not only be a blessing to you but will also be a blessing to other people, in ways you would never imagine.

If a person's passion is cooking, then his/her purpose could be to cater events, create unique recipes or host elegant sit down dinner parties, with all three options, offering a substantial profit. Please keep in mind that *there will always be an unlimited amount of avenues that will allow you to express your purpose and you can change course, at any time.* Ponder over your answers, from the "Pick Only One" self-discovery survey, and write down all the different ideas, that you can come up with, for procuring the path to your true purpose.

Another exceptional technique that you can apply, for bringing forth your core exclusive craving, is by *tuning into and trusting the inner voice* that guides you to all great things. Before beginning the easy exercise below, resolve, in advance, that the answer you seek will enter into your mind with ease and it most surely will. *Release* any mental, emotional or physical resistance, by allowing yourself to fully relax, for the next few minutes.

Now that you have freed yourself from any and all tension, *feel* from within, how *inspired* you are, *knowing* that your answer awaits you. *Believe* that you *have already received* your answer, by feeling *grateful*, from the top of your head to the tips of your toes, *acknowledging* that the ingenious inner voice, within, already knows what you are about to ask…

And it shall come to pass, that before they call, I will answer; and
while they are yet speaking, I will hear.
~ Isaiah 65:24 (K.J.V.) ~

- Find a quite room, that has a comfortable couch or chair,
  where you will not be distracted for the next 10 minutes
- Sit in an upright position with both feet lightly planted on
  the floor and let your arms lay loosely at your sides
- Close your eyes and let your lids become very relaxed
- Take five deep breaths, by inhaling and exhaling slowly
  through your nostrils
- Bring to mind, someone or something that you are truly
  grateful for
- Continue in these warm fuzzy feelings until your entire
  body is buzzing with gratitude
- After attaining a state of deep appreciation, ask your inner
  voice, "What passion should I pursue with purpose at this
  point in my life"?
- **Your answer will come through clearly in the form of
  an image or direct response**

If your answer did not come through clearly then repeat the
process a second time, with more emphasis on deepening your
relaxation level. Continue to listen carefully, to that inner voice, but
without forced effort. It is well worth your time, *if* additional
attempts are needed, to have the right answer reveal itself. *Do not
give up until it does.* If you need to, take a break and try again, when
you are ready.

When I preformed this precise exercise, back in 2002, the
image of a feather pen immediately popped into my mind. I went
into this exercise, with a completely open mind, free from any
preconceived ideas of my own, because I was excited to see what

my intuition would reveal. At that moment, it became abundantly clear to me, that the feather pen confirmed my passion and purpose to become an author.

This above all: to thine own self be true, And it must follow, as the night the day, Thou canst not then be false to any man.
~ William Shakespeare (1564-1616) ~

"Thine own self", which resides in the deepest recesses of your being, can *guide* you and *glide* you through any desired endeavor, especially **YOUR exclusive purpose**. It is imperative that you make your inner voice much more important than the loud and overbearing opinions on the outside. Nothing, outside of yourself, has the power to determine or dictate your purpose. That privilege is exclusively reserved for the inner wisdom, within each individual. *Ask* the wisdom, within, for the answers you seek, and the opportunities will always avail themselves, on the outside.

The moment your answer arrives and your perfect plan for fulfilling your purpose present's itself, you must *resist the temptation* of looking into other opportunities that have nothing to do with your purpose. *Hold fast* to your newly discovered core exclusive craving and do not let other money-making offers *rob **you*** of a minute more of your time. We know what will happen if we chase two rabbits at the same time…both *will* get away and we will be left empty handed. Aim straight at the bulls-eye and see to it that you hit your target, this time around, by *diligently* blocking out the numerous other options that surround you.

A whole new and awe-inspiring world will unfold, before your very eyes, far beyond any experience you've ever encountered, *when you take the first step,* towards lining up the things you love, for fulfilling YOUR life's purpose.

The Open Doorway from Ordinary to Extraordinary

We do not see things as they are. We see them as we are.
~ The Talmud ~

This chapter is really going to rock your world!!! The rare and radical wisdom that we are about to uncover will have you looking at life, from the highest vantage point possible. You are about to be made aware of the root reason why some people seem to have all the luck and why most people have a hard time, keeping their head above water. If turning your luck around and increasing the quality of your life is important to you, then you will especially enjoy these extraordinary insights.

The best way to ease into this powerful principle would be to share a story with you that changed my life and left a lasting impression on me.

A peaceful man, in his mid-sixties, was sitting on a park bench and soaking up the soothing sun light. He opened his eyes, when he sensed that someone was walking toward him. Standing before him was a rather rough and tough looking man, who seemed to be in a grim mood. The older gentleman asked this rather disgruntled man," Is there something I can do for you, sonny?" The young man answered back, with an aggravated undertone, "I will be moving here next week and I was wondering, "How are the people, who live here?" "That's an interesting question, my friend" but before I answer it, let me ask you a quick question, "What are the people like, where you come from?" The young man became increasingly agitated, while responding, "They are all out for themselves and the chances of running into someone nice, hardly ever happens". "Oh, I see", said the peaceful man, as he sent the traveler on his way, adding, "**You** will certainly come across the same type of people in this place".

The peaceful man resumed closing his eyes, enjoying, once again, the warmth of the sun, upon his face. He wasn't perturbed, when his deep relaxation was interrupted, yet again, by another person who desired his help. This time, standing before him was an attractive, young fellow, bearing a smile that stretched from ear to ear. The older gentleman asked this rather optimistic young man, "Is there something I can do for you, sonny?" With appreciation in his voice, the young man proceeded to say, "The company that I work for will be relocating to this area next month and I was wondering, "How are the people, who live here?" "That's an interesting question my friend" but before I answer it, let me ask you a quick question, "What are the people like where you come from?" The jovial, young man, replied, "You couldn't ask for kinder or friendlier folk, where I come from, Sir". "Oh, I see", said the peaceful man, as he sent the traveler on his way, adding, "**You** will certainly come across the same type of people in this place".

Don't let the simplicity of this story fool you, for it contains the key to reclaiming your total personal power and reestablishing your birthright to co-creation *your* **YOU-niverse!!!**

Most people have had it hammered into their head, their whole life, that "seeing is believing" but the story, above, perfectly illustrates that "believing is seeing". The man/woman, who believes that the outside world is cold and that people are cruel, will be validated by "seeing" experiences, *unfold before their eyes* that **mirror** their inner beliefs. The man/woman, who believes that the outside world is filled with wonder and that people are friendly, will be validated by "seeing" experiences, *unfold before their eyes* that **mirror** their inner beliefs.

Your personal perception is the most powerful force in your possession. It **privately** instructs the power, within, as to what you **expect** to be projected in your outer world, and so it is. Hermetic teachings tell us that "as within, so without". Full understanding and faithful application of this teaching will allow you to consistently create, *on conscious command*. This ancient principle is the most commonly misunderstood, one of them all, and therefore, we will take all the time we need, to completely comprehend its magnificent meaning.

As I mentioned in the Introduction and reiterated in the last chapter, too much technical information causes confusion and prevents people from creating the results they desire. It is your birthright to co-create, at all times, and the goal is to equip you with air tight steps, to get you started as soon as possible. As always, I will continue to state all reference sources, whenever applicable and I highly recommend that you take the time to extend your studies, on your own, if you hunger to know the history of any topics in particular. Having said that, and for the time being, we will be firmly factual, for the next few pages.

As above, so below; As below, so above; As within, so without;
As without, so within.
~ Hermes Trismegistus ~

The universe is inside of you and you are inside of the universe. Most people know that they have their existence, within the universe, but very few are aware that the vastness of the universe is inside of them. The world is inside of you and you are inside the world. We have lost touch with our true source, as we find ourselves getting pulled out of our personal power because of our constant clock watching and "counting down the days" conduct. Quantum Mechanics and Classical Physicists have gone to great lengths to provide us with sufficient proof that we are, in no way, detached or disconnected from the outside world.

The Esoteric Agenda, readily available to everyone with Internet access, is a series of online video documentaries, providing us with exceptional precision, scientific evidence that explains our connection to all things, in existence. Follow along closely, as we condense extensive cellular research into a brief bio, so to better utilize our bantam block of time together. Quantum Mechanics enlightens us on the most fundamental known descriptions of all physical systems, at the sub-atomic level. At a cellular level, our bodies receive their impulses from the infinite universe. Initially, our cells receive this pulse from the brain. In turn, our brains receive its pulse from the heart. Serially, our hearts then receive its pulse from the earth, which ultimately receives its pulse from the ever expansive universe. *Irrevocably, everyone and everything in existence, receives their internal impulse from the very same source.*

As above, so below; As below, so above; As within, so without; As without, so within.
~ Hermes Trismegistus ~

As is in the universe so is in the earth. As is the earth so is in the universe. As is in the individual so is in the outer world. As is in the outer world so is in the individual. The power that worketh within you is your immediate connection to uniting with all physical forms that once seemed so out of reach. There is an old Chinese Proverb that says, "A picture's meaning can express ten thousand words". Do an online search for "Brain Cells and our Universe" to see, with your own eyes, that the structure or our brain is the spitting image of the structure of the universe. *Are you starting to accept that YOU are equally as amazing as the awe-inspiring universe?*

Now, going back to the internal impulses that the entire universe and everything else in existence receives from the same source, we can gain even greater clarity by going into a brief over-view of the 7 locations, within our bodies, that are receptors of these impulses, better known as the Chakra System.

The word, "chakra", is Sanskrit for "wheel". It signifies one of the seven energy centers that compose our body's entire energy system. The chakras are not physical, as they are considered to be aspects of our consciousness. In chapter 8, we discovered that all physical forms are manifested from consciousness. Consciousness can best be defined as infinite intelligence, combined with endless energy that produces physical and rapid results, on command. The chakra system serves to harmonize us with a sense of balance, well-being and wholeness.

According to the Esoteric Agenda – Part 8 – Illusions & Reality, that is available for you to view, on various websites over the internet, informs us that the 7 chakras are as follows:

The Root Chakra
The Sacral Chakra
The Solar Plexus Chakra
The Heart Chakra
The Throat Chakra
The Third Eye Chakra
The Crown Chakra

There are several attributes assigned to each chakra, such as color, element, function, etc. You can learn more about these components by studying several of the color-coded chakra charts that are available online. Our sole focus will be on the locations of these 7 chakras because, keep in mind, there is an all-powerful conclusion that we are aiming to arrive at and will be, momentarily!!!

After studying twenty different versions of the color-coded chakra charts, I am able to give you general guidance on the focal points for the 7 chakras, as follows:

The Root Chakra is located in the coccyx perineum region.
The Sacral Chakra is located in the sacrum region.
The Solar Plexus Chakra is located in the stomach region.
The Heart Chakra is located in the centre of our chest.
The Throat Chakra is located in the throat region.
The Third Eye Chakra is located between the brows.
The Crown Chakra is located at the top of our head.

Although there are different variations of the chakra chart, they all share the same common element in that all of the colors, representing the locations of our 7 focal points, are positioned perfectly down the center, and spaced apart, at equal distance.

According to the Esoteric Agenda – Part 8 – Illusions & Reality, "Our earth also has 7 chakras at equally distant locations from one another". The same way our bodies receive energy from the 7 focal points, the body of the Living Earth requires energy and receives its life force through 7 specific focal points as well. It is also a known fact that our world has 7 continents. The Esoteric Agenda further informs us of the distinct locations and continents of the earth's 7 chakra points, as follows:

The Root Chakra is located in Mount Shasta, California (North America)

The Sacral Chakra is located in Lake Titicaca, Peru/Bolivia (South America)

The Solar Plexus Chakra is located in Ulura Kata Tjuta, Australia (Australia)

The Heart Chakra is located in Glastonbury or Shaftsbury England (Europe)

The Throat Chakra is located in Great Pyramids of Giza, Egypt (Africa)

The Third Eye Chakra is located Kuh-e-Malek Siah, Iran (Middle East)

The Crown Chakra is located Mount Kailas, Tibet (Asia)

After researching these locations individually, in connection to our 7 continents, I discovered that the Third Eye chakra is indicated as being in the Middle East, which means that there aren't any chakras in the Antarctica area. I continued my investigation and came across a very interesting article called "Earth Chakras" by expert, Robert Coon, on www.weavings.co.uk, which explains that the Third Eye Chakra is mobile and moves around, whereas the other 6 chakras are fixed in stable locations.

As above, so below; As below, so above; As within, so without; As without, so within.
~ Hermes Trismegistus ~

"As above, so below; As below, so above". If you searched online, like I suggested, for visual validation between the human cerebral cortex and the make up of our universe, you can clearly see that the circuit pathways are strikingly the same. "As within, so without; As without, so within". *If you take the time to self-study the human chakra system and the earth chakra system, you can come to the inspiring conclusion that our inner body is the mirror image of the outer world.* This supreme knowledge should be enough for you to hold yourself in the highest regard and understand your unlimited potential as a human being.

When the **workings of your inner world** become more mesmerizing to you than the outside world, you can "bet your bottom dollar" that the outside world will, in turn, reveal your most riveting ideas and ideals, by presenting you with their physical manifestations.

Now…continue to pay close attention because I am about to sanction you with "the secret" that everyone is searching for, while tightly tying together what I've been saying here:

> It's not them, it's **you**.
> It's not there, it's **here**.
> It's not then, it's **now**.
> ~ Author Unknown ~

These 3 straight-to-the-point statements are what we all have longed to hear, our whole lives while, at the same time, this truth fills us with fear because we have been programmed to believe that personal responsibility is a burden. On one hand, we are afraid to stand on our own two feet and yet, on the other hand, we yearn to be free to live life on our own terms. The truth will set you free and your freedom lies in taking back your personal power by reclaiming total responsibility for your life.

We have been watching people play the "blame-game" since the day we were born and erroneously, over time, this fallacious belief became ingrained into us, as well. We've been repeatedly told that outside forces would see to it that we fall flat on our faces, whenever we attempt to break free from mediocrity. As easy as it has been to blame other people for our obstacles and unseen forces for our past failures, your personal power is much too big of a price to pay. Besides, you are on the brink of making your mind accept the reality that **<u>YOU</u> *are* a force to be reckoned with!!!** You no longer need to be afraid that you may fail, in achieving any future ambitions, because you now have ground-breaking knowledge and a fast-acting formula, in your arsenal.

Let's take a closer look at the 3 straight-to-the-point statements and consider how they can take our lives from *ordinary to extraordinary*, in just a matter of days.

Straight-to-the-point statement 1 out of 3:
It's not them, it's **you**.

The story, that started this chapter, simply states that *you will always attract the encounters, events and experiences that you expect*. What we expect, within the inner, invisible realm inside of ourselves, is precisely what the power, within, will project on the outside screen of the world. If you expect to come into contact with wonder people, places and things, then, you will. If you expect to be confronted by problematic people, places and things, then, you will. *YOU have complete control over people, places and things that surround you through the power of your perception.* You can continue to allow everything that you see going on in the outside world, determine your beliefs and dictate your direction **or** you can change your beliefs to be self-supportive and therefore, all together alter what you will see unfold, in your sacred space.

You may have unconsciously attracted co-workers or acquaintances that annoy you, day in and day out, **but** you have the power to omit them from your life. Have you ever thought that maybe your spirit is trying to move you into starting up your own business, or pushing you to pursue a profession that revolves around your true purpose? All of us, at one time or another, have had such thoughts, shoving them aside, as "unattainable dreams", when, in fact, it's really been our own lack of knowledge, meshed with our fear based beliefs that have stopped us, in our tracks.

155

Quantum Physics and the Law of Attraction certify that everything in existence has a natural vibration to it. The two primary emotions that we experience, from which every other emotion branches out of, are fear and love. Your mind was wired to receive wisdom from infinite intelligence and your body was brilliantly designed to receive endless energy. The physical world is a manifestation of infinite intelligence and endless energy. You block the flow for infinite intelligence and endless energy to fill you up with everything you need to create your dream-like life when you operate from fear. Anything that is placed before you, that stirs up a feeling of fear, is intended for you to conquer inwardly. <u>Face your fears, by tapping into your highest human potential</u>. The goal is to get rid of fear and let love in, to manifest at the speed of light!!!

Mile by mile, it's a trial. Yard by yard, it's hard. Inch by inch, it's a cinch.

~ Unknown ~

If you are miserable, where you work, unfulfilled with what you do for a living, and do not naturally get along with the people you work with, then start working the steps, this week, by manifesting a much more meaningful environment. When you do what you *love*, the *wealth* will follow, but when you do what you *dread*, out of *fear*, you will continue to live "paycheck to paycheck" and barely get by. If you find yourself, feeling a bit overwhelmed, in taking those first steps, let me reassure you that feeling overwhelmed is an extension of *fear*, that you have power over, and there is no reason to do anything drastic that would make you dive off the deep edge. *Focus* on the first step and you'll find that the second step will be a breeze. If you can not afford to be out of work for one week, then your first step would be to use "The Unspoken Formula to Fast Fortunes" to call forth a supplemental income.

You may manifest an opportunity that pays you a little less or then again, maybe more than you are making now and if it covers the bills, then *go for it*. Nothing is set in stone. You may have to make one or two more minor changes, before settling into your perfect place, for your perfect pay. The most important thing, to keep in mind, is that you are freeing yourself up, to feel the happiness that has been hidden in your heart, and allowing that happiness to put you in tune, with the powerful vibration of love. Your high vibrations of happiness will allow you to perpetually manifest the life you love. You have got to start, sometime, and you have got to start, somewhere. "Inch by inch, it's a cinch and like I always say, "Now" is "how", so stay in the day".

Straight-to-the-point statement 2 out of 3:
It's not there, it's **here**.

In the previous chapter, it was revealed to us, by the late Jules Renard, that everything we want, is waiting for us to ask, and everything we want, also wants us. Our wants will appear, out there, as soon as we *find* the feeling of fulfillment, inside of ourselves. Typically, we tend to perceive that what we want, will be ours on a different day, other than the one we are actually living in…. the here and now. With this kind of perception, it's no wonder that our *wants* are projected *out* of our present reality. From the minute we bounce out of bed, we are projecting that the day will be the same, as the one before, and we mentally start rehearsing our regular routines.

Every encounter, event and experience you could ever enjoy, happens to be at hand, right here and right now. You must initiate your imagination, from having your *wants* projected, *out there*, by picturing yourself as *already having* what you want, right *here*. The only reason why you haven't gotten what you've wanted is because you keep picturing it to be, *out there* ,and you keep believing that it will not manifest for a few days, weeks, months or years. You can stop bending over backwards and burning yourself out when you invest that energy into mastering your mental images.

The tangible things of this world were made manifest from intangible consciousness. Most people have their conscious mind made up that **one day**, all of their **hard work** will pay off. Sadly, the wealth that they desire never seems to make its way into their wallets. As challenging as it may appear to be, at this moment, you must resolve, within your conscious mind, that when you tap into your inner intelligence and express your energy, through activities of endearment, only then will manifesting all forms of physical matter, be brought to life, as if by magic!

* <u>M</u>astering <u>A</u>wareness <u>G</u>uarantees <u>I</u>mmediate <u>C</u>reation *

What physical object are you holding in your hands, right here and now?

This book is comprised of molded matter, physically manifested from my consciousness, allowing me to tap into infinite intelligence, so to receive my information and be supplied with an endless stream of energy to carrying me through to completion.

1. It was not difficult for me to make the conscious decision, to commit to creating this book, but if I skipped this *simple* but ever so essential step, this physical copy could not exist.

2. It was easy to determine that this book would be about manifesting because Metaphysics is my all time favorite subject, but if I skipped this *simple* but ever so essential step, this physical copy could not exist.

3. It was effortless to envision everything that I desired to discuss throughout this book, but if I skipped this *simple* but ever so essential step, this physical copy could not exist.

4. It was exciting to lose total track of time, while I wailed away at the keyboard, but if I skipped this *simple* but ever so essential step, this physical copy could not exist.

In a minute, you will *know* that the simple steps, above, are as easy as I am making them out to be, when you identify the fatal flaw that everyone makes, when working with their imagination, regarding manifestation.

I am Alpha and Omega, the beginning and the end, the first and the last.
~ Revelation 22:13 (K.J.V.) ~

It is not a mistake that "the beginning and the end" make no mention of being "the middle". The "beginning" is the intangible idea and the "end" is the physical formation. The middle is "who, what, where, when and how". Various visualization techniques teach us to close our eyes and see our imagery-self, successfully completing each step, from start to finish, before physically taking any action. We are then told to mix in as much detail as possible, and play with as many mental images as it takes, to make our mini-mental-movie as perfect as possible. It's only after we are completely satisfied with our edited edition, that we are then instructed to replay our mental movies, over and over, in our minds, until such time, we manifest it into reality.

But when ye pray, use not vain repetitions, as the heathen do: for they think that they shall be heard for their much speaking.
~Matthew 6:7 (K.J.V.) ~

Not only is repetition, absolutely futile, but equally pointless is that nearly everyone gets lost in the loop hole of imagining "*how*" they see themselves, *acquiring* the object of their desire. They waste all of their time, stuck in the "middle" and never arrive at the "end" of *already receiving their desire*. For instance, "The Unspoken Formula to Fast Fortunes", began as an intangible idea in my mind. I *skipped* right over the middle, and I immediately *imagined* myself, physically holding the paperback version of my book in the palm of my hands. I *pictured* my book as being placed on the coffee tables, at all of my close friends and family members' houses. Last but not least, I *visualized* my book, on the Best Sellers shelf, at all the brand name bookstores. When you go directly to the end of your resolve, once the initial intangible idea surfaces, the "middle" will fill in, on its own, as quickly as a boat, with a hole, fills up with water.

Now, bring to mind, both of my Movado watch manifestations: As soon as I *desired* the first watch, I *skipped straight to imagining* it on my wrist and *never wasted time*, visualizing anything but the physical object as already being in my possession. The same amount of mental work went into manifesting the second watch. Do not waste your precious time or energy on visualizing yourself as "getting" what you want. Instead, give yourself the guarantee that you've "got it" by imagining that **IT IS ALREADY HERE** and that you are happy, **NOW**, in owning it, outright.

Straight-to-the-point statement 3 out of 3:
It's not then, it's **now**.

The invisible realm, where your inner being resides, is not concerned with the time on the clock or the date on the calendar. Human beings have the luxury of getting lost in thought because we desire and require relaxation. However, it should give you great comfort to know that each and every moment is of the utmost importance, for the singular source that all things receive their life force from. The power, which worketh within you, concentrates its infinite intelligence and compresses its endless energy, in the *now*, to make it possible that purposeful feats are fueled with the necessary force, for completion.

The "moment at hand" is continuously on high alert, to those individuals, who place priority in figuring out how to make instant, conscious contact, in order to intentionally co-create the unique YOU-niverse, entrusted to them.

Inside of YOU, is the ***power to do***, exceeding abundantly above all that you ask, think, or can even imagine, in this lifetime!!! The only thing that is expected of you is to pick one or more, most meaningful outcomes, that you *genuinely expect to manifest*, and **then totally trust** that, "NOW" knows "HOW", to make it happen. The "moment at hand" is of the utmost importance! *Tap into this very moment*, so you can **start** "reaping the rewards" of enjoying, impressive and unwavering increase to the quality of **YOUR LIFE**.

Reinforcing the Simple Six Steps to Fast Fortunes

The man who acquires the ability to take full possession of his own mind may take possession of anything else to which he is justly entitled.
~ Andrew Carnegie (1835-1919) ~

We have uncovered so much, in such a short amount of time!!! Repetition will make remembering and mastering everything we've learnt about manifesting, sink into our subconscious mind, twice as fast. It would, in no way, be waste of your time, to reread this book, from start to finish, if you require reinforcement, or you can take the shortcut and study this chapter, so to better establish a rock solid belief system. Think of this chapter as a complete refresher course that will allow you instant access to all of the key points that you can put into practice immediately.

The Six Simple & Straightforward Exclusive Steps for Fortunes:

1. *KNOW* that **you** *CAN* have *ANYTHING* your heart desires.
2. *Describe every detail* of your desire, out loud or on paper.
3. *Make up your mind* that you *WILL* get what you want.
4. *Fine tune your feelings* by establishing a state of certainty.
5. *Follow all actions* you are gravitated towards.
6. *Take over ownership* of your heart's desire.

Simple & Straightforward Step 1 out of 6:

1. *KNOW* that **you** *CAN* have *ANYTHING* your heart desires.

There are 4-phases that we are all destined to graduate from, in order to earn the education and experience to co-create with ease:

The 1st phase is where all we do is *doubt*, and taking any action is out of the question, at this point. We doubt that we have any say as to what our destiny will be and doubt that we have the power to make a difference in our own lives or in the world at large.

The 2nd phase is where all we do is *think*, but we are still not quite ready to take any action. We start seeking out stories of other people who have succeeded in designing the lifestyle they love and we start to think that maybe we have what it takes to direct our own destiny. We are much more open minded, at this point, about the possibility of turning our dreams into reality.

The 3rd phase is where we begin to *believe* that we have what it takes to succeed and start taking baby steps to get what we want. We believe that if we work hard and think as positive as possible, we will eventually get everything we are after. We are well on our way to co-creating our picture perfect world but we still struggle with some of our old beliefs that significantly slows down our progress.

The 4th phase is when we start to *know* that manifesting our dreams and desires was never meant to be difficult. We did everything, on our end, to cast out all doubts, thoughts, and beliefs, that once stood in our way. Now, we not only *know* that it is our birthright to co-create our dream-like life but we are actively manifesting one desire after another.

Even if everyone else decides to stay stuck in phase 1, 2 or 3, you owe it to yourself to *KNOW* that **you** *CAN* have *ANYTHING* your heart desires. The only thing that could keep you from establishing **your certainty** would be by waiting for the people that surround you, to start expressing theirs first. You were born to be a co-creator…not a waitor. Do not doubt, for a single second, that you can't have what you want, when it is *even easier* to KNOW that **you** CAN.

Simple & Straightforward Step 2 out of 6:

2. *Describe every detail* of your desire, out loud or on paper.

In much the same way we require specific directions to a friend's house, which we're visiting for the first time, the power, within, will need for you to be as specific as possible. Would you go out of your way, tracking down your friend's house, if the only information he/she provided you was the town that he/she lived in? It could easily take weeks, months or years to track down your friend, depending upon the size of the town! However, when your friend supplies you with an actual address, such as "123 Smith Street, Bumble Bee, Mississippi", your search time is significantly reduced. Accordingly, you would get there even quicker, if you are also given detailed driving directions.

You can only stake claim on what you want, when you know, exactly what you want. The desires of your heart are yours and yours alone to decide. All of the details are inside of you, so seek the wisdom, from within, for specifications that make your spirit sing and bring happiness to your heart. You are not to concern yourself with dollars and cents or contemplate other options that could cost less than your distinct desires.

We are told, in Deuteronomy 4:2, not to add to or take away, "from the Word". The desires of your heart are those words, spoken from the wisdom, within. If you desire something specific, do not add on fancy features, used to impress other people. On the other hand, stand firm in refusing to settle for second best. You must be prepared to say NO to what you do NOT want, if some sort of similar substitute appears on your path, prior to the attainment of your true desire. This type of diversion will only take place, if your firm decision is sprinkled with doubt, so you need to strengthen your resolve, if this situation occurs. By doing so, you triple the speed of your delivery. You already *KNOW* that **you**

CAN have *ANYTHING*, your heart desires, and now you can confidently describe those desires, in detail, because you will not be denied.

Simple & Straightforward Step 3 out of 6:

3. *Make up your mind* that you *WILL* get what you want.

The primary reason why most people are afraid to wrap their mind around manifesting something specific is because they might miss out on something even bigger and better. This is a subconscious safety defense mechanism that is designed to protect that person from possibly being disappointed and having their heart broken, if their dream does not come true. Ironically, this very belief is what actually keeps these people in a perpetual state of disappointment and heartbreak, questioning *why* their dreams have not already come true.

Now that we have acknowledged that the power, within, is able to abundantly exceed all that we ask or think, we know in advance that we will never be disappointed when we take ownership of our desire. You will miss out on manifesting, altogether, if you do not get started on something specific and consistently increase your collection, as you go. "Picking" then "sticking", is the name of the game.

For each and every excuse that could crop up, as to why you can't have what you want, fire back with five reassuring reasons for why you WILL get what you want. Enough is enough with the excuses!!! The path will be paved out brilliantly, on our behalf, every time we exercise our right to make definite decisions. As co-creators, we are responsible in stating precisely what we want, without wavering or worrying about "who, what, where, when and how". Our rightful role is to *make up our mind* that we *WILL* get what we want and *know* that our resolute decision is all that is required of us to "seal the deal."

I would like to share with you an exciting experience that happened to me, just this past week, proving how truly powerful our definite decisions are, when we remain unwavering in our convictions. I have always been big into name-brand clothes and I will not talk myself out of buying a fifty dollar rinky-dinky tank top, if I absolutely love it. I spent the last few weeks, putting together an order for 9 extremely expensive t-shirts, fashioned by an exclusive designer that I absolutely adore. On Monday night, I *made up my mind* that I could care less about how much I would have to pay, to complete my order, because deep down, I truly desired these specific t-shirts. I cleared my conscience, regarding the outrageous cost of my order, by reciting a quote that I wrote a few years ago:

I'm not going to worry...I'm not going to fear...I'm just going to jump and the net WILL appear.
~ Jamie L. Briggs ~

I knew that if I would be willing to spend this much money on something that I whole-heartedly desired, then the money would appear, as it always does, whenever I refuse to waver on my definite decisions. All apprehension was freed from my mind, the minute I made my definite decision. The following afternoon, I received a text message, from my good friend, saying that she had a surprise for me and would give it to me, when we met up later that evening. *What do you think my unexpected surprise was that night?*

Get a load of this...my friend's father owns a shop and he had several t-shirts left over, that he was looking to free up from his stock. My friend asked her father if she could give them to me, as a gift, because she knew that this name-brand was, by far, my favorite. After sorting through the selection of sizes, I went home that Tuesday night with 7 new cool and colorful t-shirts, by the designer that I absolutely adore. Less than 24 hours, after making my definite decision, I received my heart's desire. You will be able to manifest just as fast, when you quickly come to terms that *making up your mind* that you *WILL* get what you want, is the most primitive part of the entire process.

Simple & Straightforward Step 4 out of 6:

4. *Fine tune your feelings* by establishing a state of certainty.

If your old beliefs are causing you to doubt your birthright to freely co-create the intimate space that you inhibit, then chances are you will struggle with your certainty, while attempting to manifest. You can easily overcome this potential obstacle by knowing *what* the title of co-creator entails, and by staying true to your rightful responsibilities, while allowing the power, within, to perform its primary functions.

Everything you could ever hope to get your hands on already exists, either in a physical or imaginary form. All things, currently in physical form, initially began as an intangible idea in someone's imagination, or from some unseen source. Everyone and everything, in existence, receives its impulse and life force from the same source. Everyone and everything, in existence, is embedded with their own unique set of heart-felt desires. In much the same way that a strawberry seed contains the code to bring forth a full fledge strawberry bush, our desires contain the code to making them manifest, just as easily and efficiently. You can spend your whole life interviewing the billions of people that occupy our planet, and you will never come across two people who have identical desires.

YOUR heart-felt desires were intended for **YOU** to make manifest, over the course of **your** lifetime. You can counteract every excuse that could come up, for why you can't have what you want, when you realize that **it is your right and your responsibility to bring them to life**. If you fail to act on the opportunities to manifest, when the inspiration strikes, then the spirit will arouse this desire in someone else, who will. How many times have you heard other people say, "They stole my idea!!" If we do not take action when, we are instructed to, from this wisdom, within ourselves, then someone else will reap the rewards that could have been ours, and we have no one else to blame but ourselves.

It is time to stop questioning our worthiness to co-create and depriving ourselves of the things that we love. The life force is the love source that will always pave a path for us to merge with the things that we love, when we rid our consciousness, of fear. The power, within, could never and would never keep you from the things you love. Your clouded and confused consciousness, brought about from decades of contradicting conditioning, has kept you from clearly seeing that the way was available all along.

As a co-creator, the majority of your work will be mental and includes completely clearing your consciousness, from all doubt. Your consciousness is the doorway that your desires will enter into your world. You will start by becoming crystal clear about what you truly want. Next, you will mentally face all fear, by preparing for the worst *but* expecting the best. Make up your mind that you are prepared to pay any price and that you willing to do whatever it takes, to honor your heart's desire. Now.... *say it*, like you *really* mean it…**"I am prepared to pay any price and willing to do whatever it takes, to honor my heart's desire, because I deserve it!!!"**

You DO deserve to have ALL of your hearts desires for the simple fact that you were born to be a happy human being.

When you speak that statement, aloud or inwardly, with all of your mental might, the power, within, will instantly receive your feeling-infused request and you will have successfully fulfilled your part of the process, by clearing your consciousness of all apprehensions. The very same second that you *establish this state of certainty*,

169

you can know that the manifestation cycle officially started and kicked straight into high gear.

Simple & Straightforward Step 5 out of 6:

5. *Follow all actions* you are gravitated towards.

The still small voice, from within, is only hard to hear when your conscience is cluttered and cramped with worry. As soon as you arrive at your definite decision, by rising above all apprehensions, your certainty will be established and instantaneously flip your intuition, from "off" to "on". As surely as summer follows spring, you will be given guidance from within, after you courageously affirm, **"I am prepared to pay any price and willing to do whatever it takes to honor my heart's desire, because I deserve it!!!"** If you are crystal clear and sincere, when saying that you are willing to do whatever it takes, you will be delighted to discover that *all actions you are gravitated towards* are easier than you ever could have imagined.

On Monday night, when I *made up my mind* that I was going to get the extremely expensive t-shirts that I desired, I had every intention of placing my order and paying out of pocket, first thing the following morning. When I woke up on Tuesday, my intuition told me to hold off for one more day, assuring me that it would be worth the wait, until Wednesday, to process my transaction. As motivated as I was, now that my mind was made up, I knew that there would be no harm in holding off for only one more day and I had no doubt that my intuition knew what it was doing. That Tuesday night, when my good friend generously gifted me all those t-shirts, the feelings of utter amazement and gratitude made manifesting my heart's desire that much more meaningful than simply saving all that money.

Learning to tune into and trust your intuition will become second nature when you see how much clarity comes from completely clearing your conscience, by making definite decisions. Your intuition will figure out the "who, what, where, when and how". Discipline yourself to describe your desires, in detail, and then immediately fast-forward to foreseeing yourself as already possessing the physical manifestation. Believing is receiving and inspires your intuition to follow through until all faith infused requests are fulfilled.

Simple & Straightforward Step 6 out of 6:

6. *Take over ownership* of your heart's desire.

Expect the unexpected and prepare to be pleasantly surprised with the wonderful ways, your heart's desires will manifest. This is the step that co-creators spend most of their time, trying to figure out, but it is not our role to coordinate or orchestrate the plans. You will certainly be at the right place, at the right time, to receive your heart's desire *if* you remain true to you rightful responsibilities.

There is no way to determine what route the wisdom, within, will walk you on, in receipt of your heart's desire. The reason why you are considered a co-creator is because it was never intended that you do it all alone, nor should you want to, when the life force and love source, within you, are the inner promptings, insisting to expand enjoyment... through you. When you play your part of paying attention to detail and not doubting in your heart that your requests have been readily received, the wisdom, within, will directly lead you to your desire every time.

Take two minutes to write down, on an index card, the **Re-phrased Version # 1** of Hebrews 11:1 that we revised in Chapter 4, which *are* the <u>**fail-proof instructions**</u> for converting invisible ideas into physical matter and dwell on it, whenever you are wrestling with doubt:

Now <u>certainty</u> *is* the <u>physical matter that molds</u> our heart's desire, the *confirmation* that <u>we will see</u> what was *initially an invisible idea* in our mind.

Doubt will stop you from ever getting started and needs to be quickly "cast out" of your consciousness. **Certainty will guarantee** that you take over ownership of that which you yearn for and needs to be "called forth", as soon as possible. In the next chapter, I will provide you with the most effective 3-minute formula for expelling *doubt* and instilling *certainty*.

Let's retrace several of the steps that we previously took and perfectly package everything together so that you can start making your desires manifest with next-to-no resistance:

- ALL things ARE possible to him *that* **believes**
- According to YOUR faith, be it ***done unto*** YOU
- Faith *is* the **substance** of things hoped for, the <u>*evidence of things not seen*</u>
- Things which are **seen** were *not* made of things which **do appear**
- I girded you, though you have **not known** me
- Now unto him that *is* able to do <u>**exceeding abundantly above all that we ask or think**</u>, *according* to **the power that worketh in us**

Who could possibly continue to remain unconscious of their right to co-create after receiving such splendid knowledge???

Your guess is as good as mine as to why the world would teach us that manifesting our most minuet dreams are beyond our reach when the truth is, we are always but one belief away, from acquiring our wildest wishes. Out of all of the theories about how our universe and world came into existence, one thing is for certain…human hands had no involvement in the initial act of creation. "Things which are **seen** were *not* made of things which **do appear**", therefore, if there is anything that you would like to manifest in the fastest time frame possible, then you are going to get comfortable with the fact that faith is the answer.

Faith is the only force on earth that is powerful enough to instantaneously covert intangible ideas into tangible items.

Which would you prefer…to know the "who, what, where, when and how", your desires will happen *or* to actually **have** them happen, because you can't have both. The "need to know in advance" is a confirmation of doubt, designed to completely cancel out the mighty mechanics of faith. You must have total trust that your definite decision *will manifest*, by skipping over the middle, and mentally seeing yourself as already in possession of the object you desire.

Believing in the best and receiving the best will not drain you, the way that incessant worrying and doubting does. You can stop burning the candle, at both ends, when you are willing to simply eliminate "doubting your dreams away", by exchanging those doubts with, "Faith *is* the **substance** of things hoped for, the _evidence of things not seen._" It is time to dust off your dreams and let them come to life, knowing that ALL things ARE possible to him *that* **believes**.

The doubts of others have no power in preventing your desires from manifesting because, "According to YOUR faith, be it **done unto** YOU." The world desperately needs people, wise enough to turn their backs on doubt, as they tap into their power, from within, substantiating that **dreams do come true.** Faith has the power to move mountains and miraculously manifest dreams without strain or stress. *Can you honestly say,* upon hearing how easy it was for me to manifest 7 extremely expensive t-shirts, including the other numerous manifestations I've cited that you are still willing to work overtime when your desires can be ***done unto*** YOU with very little effort on your end???

You can go on believing that physical force is the answer but you will only start seeing rapid results when you realize that the universe is made up of conscious, living, and intelligent energy. All matter is ruled by what it is made up of, and when we master our own minds, we can consciously call forth, anything and everything we so desire. As established in Genesis 1:28, human beings have been given dominion over all things of a material nature. Set out to direct your most desirable thoughts, with unwavering intention, and watch how quickly, you can materialize that which you wish to manifest into your world.

Up until recently, you've lacked the essential knowledge that the *force and source of all creation is always with you,* for you have been led astray by others, who have not yet been made aware. You now know that the **power worketh in us** and flies into action, each time you exercise your birthright to make **distinct** decisions, affirming that you undeniably deserve to have your heart's desire.

The impersonal power that *is* able to do **<u>exceeding abundantly above all that we ask or think</u>** can only operate *after* a conscious co-creator speaks something **specific** into existence. The manifestation cycle does not work the other way around as it is a violation to the free will that was generously given to you. Refuse anyone or anything, outside of yourself, to dictate the design of your life. Break free from the unconscious fear that expressing your free will is some sort of sin, and start being the bona fide co-creator that you were born to be.

You were born with the built-in blueprint to create your unique universe, in the same way that the unseen source created the ultimate universe. Despite being taught to dismiss your dreams and being told that it is blasphemy to believe in yourself, **you <u>do have</u> the final say, concerning how you live your life.** Are you actually going to continue allowing yourself to be directed by others, who know significantly less than you do and go out of their way to prevent others from activating their own powerful principle of faith? **There is nothing that can stop you** from salvaging your certainty and getting into the swing of co-creating all the things that would give you great joy. The sooner you start...the sooner you can have the desires of your heart!!!

Strive for Five and Ignite Your Drive

Whatever you can do, or dream you can do, begin it; boldness has
genius, power and magic in it.
~ Johann Wolfgang von Goethe (1749-1832) ~

"The Unspoken Formula to Fast Fortunes" is the master
recipe for making dreams a reality and the "Strive for Five System"
helps to determine what delicious dishes you wish to whip up, at
any given time. You are, by no means, bound to the system, set
forth in this chapter, and you will naturally get into your own
groove. However, I never liked that most books leave out a "getting started" guideline, so hence, I created the "Strive for Five
System" when I was new to the wonderful world of manifesting and
subsequently, I've always received record-breaking results. You will,
no doubt, develop your own system soon and will be able to create,
"on conscious command", when you are rightfully ready.

One of the best ways you can completely clear your mind
and make room for insightful information to enter in, with ease, is
by purging your thoughts, onto paper. *Writing is igniting* and *instant
relief is gained* by getting the things that concern us, out of our head,
by transferring them over to a piece of paper. Abraham Lincoln
knew what he was talking about when he said, "A goal properly set
is halfway reached". You will be 50% closer to achieving your goal
of financial freedom when you take the time to figure out your
"*need, freed and succeed*" numbers.

First, we will figure out your financial freedom numbers by
handwriting them in your notebook and then we will plunge into
the "Strive for Five System." It will be well worth the next half an
hour of your time, to do the written work required. You are
welcome to read through the assignments and then come back to
complete them, when you're most motivated.

The subtitle of this book is "Know & Grow Rich" because the only way you can ever expect to grow your wealth will be by knowing what you are working with, on the onset, and then determining the definite net worth that you desire to manifest, in a time frame that feels right to you. By this point in the book, you should be quite comfortable with the idea of how quickly and easily you can increase your income. Although you may not feel inspired to manifest $100K in 7 weeks and an additional $150K, only 6 months later, from winning lotto, like the lady we discussed in Chapter 7, still keep her experience, in the forefront of your mind, whenever you need confirmation that ALL things ARE possible to him/her *that* **believes**.

Any dream that you have for financial freedom *is* not only possible and probable but you can be certain that according to YOUR *faith*, it WILL be ***done unto*** you!!!

It is obvious that your "*need*" number would constitute the covering of all of your current expenses. Your "*freed*" number will not only satisfy your current expenses but will afford you a comfortable life and give you peace of mind. Your "*succeed*" number is that astronomical amount of money that you believe will solve all your problems, end all of your worries and make you feel like the luckiest person alive.

You will be amazed at how much better you will feel, after having faced your financial fears, by placing them on a piece of paper, and in front of your eyes to analyze. It will also surprise you when you realize that you can live the life you love, on a lot less money than you may presently think, at the moment. And most importantly, you will see that financial freedom is not only achievable and believable but also, your clarity will clear the way for great ideas that can instantly increase your income, to come crashing through.

Write it down. Written goals have a way of transforming wishes into wants; cant's into cans; dreams into plans; and plans into reality. Don't just think it – ink it!

~ Author Unknown ~

Get ready to flex your financial muscles and fill in the blanks below as accurately as possible:

Monthly Mortgage Payment(s): $_____ . ____

Monthly Car Payment(s): $_____ . ____

Monthly Car Insurance(s): $_____ . ____

Monthly Medical Insurance(s): $_____ . ____

Monthly Utility Bills: $_____ . ____

Monthly Credit Card Minimum(s): $_____ . ____

Monthly Grocery Expense(s): $_____ . ____

Monthly Miscellaneous Expenses: $_____ . ____

Monthly Extra Expenses: $_____ . ____

TOTAL MONTHLY EXPENSES: $_____ . ____

These 9 categories should cover every expense you currently have. You can factor your cell phone bill(s) and the approximate amount you spend on gas, etc. each month, in the Extra Expense(s) column, while maximizing the Miscellaneous Expense(s) field for emergency funds, including any additional equity line of credit or family member bill(s) that you are presently paying.

As soon as you add up all up your entire total monthly expenses on a calculator, next, divine that number by 4 to determine what your approximate weekly payments are:

Total Monthly Expenses divided by 4: $_____ . ____

Now, divide the new number above by 7 to determine what your approximate daily payments are:

Total Weekly Expenses divided by 7: $_____ . _____

After asking several homeowners who support a family of two or more members, to share their total monthly expenses with me, we were able to come up with a monthly average of $3,750.00.

If we were to divide $3,750.00 by 4 we would come up with a total weekly expense amount of $938.00. After we divide the weekly expense amount by 7 we would come up with a total daily expense amount of $134.00. We can even take it a step further and divide the daily expense amount by the average 8 hour work day to determine that a pay rate of $17.00 per hour could cover the total monthly expenses. Considering that more people work 8 hours a day, 5 days a week, you can conclude that a person, with an hourly pay rate of $23.00, is able to provide sufficient support to a multiple, family member household.

In order to figure out your financial "*need*" figure, times your total monthly expenses by 12, to determine the cost of living for a full year:

Example: $3,750.00 times 12 equals $45,000.00

Do you believe that it is possible to earn an equivalent, to your "*need*" number, by engaging in an activity that is exciting to you? If you answered, "Yes", then you are already halfway there to making that happen.

A rule of thumb for figuring out your "*freed*" number can be to double your "*need*" number or tack on an additional 25% to 50% to the total if that amount would be more then enough to lighten your load:

25 % Example: $45,000.00 times 25% equals $56,250.00
50 % Example: $45,000.00 times 50% equals $67,500.00
100% Example: $45,000.00 times 100% equals $90,000.00

Do you believe that you can quickly call forth your *"freed"* number, by making it a priority over everything else, and plugging it into the 1ˢᵗ slot of the "Strive for Five System"? If you answered, "Yes", then you are already halfway there to making that happen.

Since each person's *"succeed"* number will vary, you will want to feel your way through this figure. Do you desire a specific and steady amount of monies, per week or do you prefer lump sum payments? Would you be happy with doubling your *"freed"* number or have you always dreamt of being a millionaire? Beating around the bush or being modest is never going to get you the wealth you want, so be upfront and honest about that super-sized dollar amount, you dream about.

Do you believe that you can manifest your *"succeed"* number, by faithfully following "The Unspoken Formula to Fast Fortunes", without wavering? If you answered, "Yes", then you are already halfway there to making that happen.

It is entirely up to you, whether you wish to start manifesting your *"need"*, *"freed"* or *"succeed"* figure, first. In my opinion, doing what you love, for a living, and manifesting enough money to cover your current expenses is an excellent starting point for most people because breaking free from a lackluster life is much more satisfying than any care-free shopping spree. The thousand dollar spending excursions will come in equal proportion to your expanded prosperity consciousness. However, if you are highly motivated right now, and have complete confidence in yourself, then I say, "full steam ahead" with either your *"freed"* **or** *"succeed"* figure!!! Also, NEVER forget that it takes the same exact amount of effort to envision seeing yourself in possession of $45K as it does $100K. Take the time to think through a figure that sets your soul on fire because the power, within, has been waiting for a feeling from you that is so much stronger than the faint and fearful "barely getting by" vibrations. If Best-Selling Author and cast member of the mainstream movie, "The Secret", Dr. Joe "Mr. Fire" Vitale, can raise his vibration from "homeless" to "rich and famous", then you, too, have what it takes to drastically change the dynamics of your financial status, starting today.

Being that I've made it my mission to cover all bases, I would like to walk around one more road block before exposing the "Strive for Five System". Most people complain, day in and day out, about how much they hate having to pay bills. *Hate* is a high powered vibration that gives life to the things we focus on with feeling. Likewise, this concept also holds true for *love*, another high powered yet quite opposite vibration, giving life to the things that we focus on with feeling. While we agree that there is a vast difference between hate and love, we need to acknowledge that there is also a world of difference between mounted debt and monthly expenses.

Your newfound faith can "move mountains" of debt from your life, like it did for me, but it is unrealistic to "wish away" all reoccurring monthly bills, such as the utilities that you use every day. Wealthy people take great pride and consider it a privilege, to pay for the things that add pleasure to their life. *The truth of the matter is that people hate not knowing if* they will have enough money to pay for the bills from one month to the next. If you continue to resonate *hate*, around your expenses, then every day of each month will continue to be exhausting. *In this instant, you can choose* to appreciate the true value of the bill-paying process and experience, firsthand, how fast the funds will start flowing in, with ease.

And I will give unto thee the keys of the kingdom of heaven: and whatsoever thou shalt bind on earth shall be bound in heaven: and whatsoever thou shalt loose on earth shall be loosed in heaven.
~ Matthew 16:19 (K.J.V.) ~

The Dictionary.com definition for *heaven* is a place or state of supreme happiness. The keys to the kingdom are freely handed over to every human being who knew to track them down and they are intended to be used by us, while we are here on earth. The "Strive for Five System" completely complies with the keys for creating supreme happiness and will be explained, in elementary terms, for easy application.

We discovered in Chapter 13, the Hermetic philosophy which affirms, "As above, so below; As below, so above; and the scripture we are studying in this section is affirming, "As in Heaven, so on Earth; As on Earth, so in Heaven." Another way to look at binding and loosing would be to view it as casting out and calling forth.

To begin with: That which you cast out of your life, with your convincing words, will also be cast out of your conscience. You are then required to adapt an attitude of absolute expectancy that will subsequently force out whatever you wish to exit your environment and experience.

Likewise, that which you call forth, into your life, with your convincing words, will be enveloped, within your conscience. You are then required to adapt an attitude of absolute expectancy that will subsequently pull in whatever you wish to enter your environment and experience.

The three key words to concentrate on are *convincing, conscience* and *expectancy*. Until you are convinced that your consciousness is the fertile womb where conception starts and expectancy is the energy that masterfully molds all matter, then the mechanics of manifesting will operate at a very slow rate to accommodate *YOUR* vibration of hesitation. The more enthusiastic and excited you are, about working with the surefire formula for co-creating, the mechanics of manifesting will then operate at a very rapid rate, to accommodate YOUR vibration of anticipation. *Do you still doubt that YOU ARE the leading authority over your life?*

Now, let's review the list that you generated, by completing the exercise at the end of Chapter 11, "Procuring Your Passions and Wildest Wishes". The goal is to have a minimum of 20 deep-seated dreams and desires, to make this your best year yet. We will be working in groups of 5 or less depending upon your comfort level and you can develop your list of 20, over time, but in the meantime, you will need at least 5, to start off with.

It has been brought to my attention that whenever someone is granted 3 wishes, his/her third wish is always for more wishes, which is why I find that striving for 5, at a time, is enough to awaken our latent powers, without feeling overwhelmed. You are welcome to work on one, two or three desires, at a time, and work your way up, for as long as it takes, so to familiarize yourself with the functions of the formula. Ultimately, *you will want to strive,* juggling more, but it is not advised that you attempt more than 5, because you then run the risk of short-fusing your forces.

Look at your list and select the top 5 things that would bring supreme happiness to your heart, upon their unfolding. In due time, you will decide if the items that remain on your list will be made manifest or replaced with updated desires. In the meantime, the task at hand is to pick the 5 most important things that jump off the page, begging to be brought to life, over the others. Now, feel your way through the top 5 and put them, in order of importance, with 1 being the most important and 5 as being the feeblest from the list. Once you have your priorities in place, your gut will guide you as to whether you should focus fully on one or more of your desires, by taking into consideration, your comprehension of the concepts as well as the magnitude of the manifestations you have selected.

There is no order that's too tall and you truly can have it all but there is no shame in starting small. If you feel any resistance from within, when you come to the third or fourth item on your list, then that is your intuition telling you to start with and stick with the first two, for the time being. You will always want to tune into and trust your intuition because it knows you better than anyone else in this world ever will. Also keep in mind that the "Strive for Five System" is a blueprint for anyone who is unsure of where to begin but if your intuition inspires and instructs you to approach manifesting from a different angle, then it is wise to trust your instincts.

The keys to the kingdom of heaven tell us that we can dead bolt the doorway, where *fears and dreads* reside, within the confines of our minds, while unlocking the entryway that leads to our dreams, via the power of our words. Every day conversation will confirm that "what" you say is not nearly as important as "how" you say it. You must start becoming conscious that your words carry weight and your dominant feelings create the physical outcome from this combined force-field. *When you consciously cast out what you do not want and consciously call forth what you do want, from a stance of complete conviction, you will never be denied the end result you expect.* We are told to come boldly to the throne, in Hebrews 4:16, and told to make our requests known, in Philippians 4:6. **You have got to be bold if you expect it to unfold!!!**

This is the 3-minute formula for *casting out* and *calling forth* which can be applied by writing, reciting with mental might or spoken out loud, with certainty, but be ever so conscious of the weight that your words carry. Internally insist that your intention make an immediate impact and impression in your present reality. Always speak the following formula with full sincerity, focus and feeling:

Line 1 of 5:
I CAST OUT ALL BELIEFS, FEELINGS AND THOUGHTS ABOUT (<u>FILL IN THE BLANK</u>).

Line 2 of 5:
I AM DONE WITH (<u>FILL IN THE BLANK</u>).

Line 3 of 5:
I CALL FORTH ALL BELIEFS, FEELINGS AND THOUGHTS ABOUT (<u>FILL IN THE BLANK</u>).

Line 4 of 5:
ACCORDING TO MY FAITH IT IS DONE UNTO ME AND THEREFORE I NOW KNOW THAT IT IS DONE.

Line 5 of 5:
I AM (FILL IN WITH A FEELING THAT CAPTURES THE ESSENSE OF THIS EXPERIENCE) TO BE (FILL IN WITH YOUR DEFINITE DECISION).

Here is an example using a financial freedom figure of $45K that a person desires to manifest from specifically freelancing Notary services:

I CAST OUT ALL BELIEFS, FEELINGS AND THOUGHTS ABOUT EMPLOYEE DEPENDANCY.

I AM DONE WITH WORKING FOR SOMEBODY ELSE.

I CALL FORTH ALL BELIEFS, FEELINGS AND THOUGHTS ABOUT SUCCEEDING AS AN INDEPENDENT NOTARY.

ACCORDING TO MY FAITH IT IS DONE UNTO ME AND THEREFORE I NOW KNOW THAT IT IS DONE.

I AM GRATEFUL TO BE GENERATING ABOVE AND BEYOND $45K BEFORE THE END OF THIS YEAR, FROM STAMPING MY NOTARY SEAL, AND SIGNING MY NAME TO DOCUMENTS THAT ARE IMPORTANT TO OTHER PEOPLE.

Notice that all of the power principles are perfect wrapped into this 3-minute formula and leaves no room for failure or guessing games. Not only does the last statement expect exceeding accomplishment but it incorporates the appropriate feeling and fast forwards to the devotion as already being in motion. Paying attention to detail and seeing yourself as already in possession of your proclamations, are enough to ensure that the power, within, will provide the perfect plan, for fulfillment. Since *certainty* is your guarantee, make sure that you meditate on your custom-created 3-minute formula for casting out and calling forth, for as long as it takes to completely consume your consciousness.

As much manifesting as I have done, over the past two decades, I still sometimes rely on the "Strive for Five System" when my busy schedule has my mind scattered in several different directions, and I need a format that will force me to sharpen my focus. My method for effectively executing the "Strive for Five System" and receiving astonishing results is as follows:

1. Select the 5 desires that mean the most to you, at this moment
2. Write down a custom *cast out* and *call forth* index card, for every desire
3. Silently read over the 1st index card then close your eyes and feel the physical sensation of this desire as being YOUR reality
4. Verbally speak the last line with sincerity, certainty and intention

5. Now, enhance the feeling that captures the essence of this experience while speaking out loud, "IT IS DONE"

6. Silently read over the 2nd index card then close your eyes and feel the physical sensation of this desire as being YOUR reality

7. Verbally speak the last line with sincerity, certainty and intention

8. Now, enhance the feeling that captures the essence of this experience while speaking out loud, "IT IS DONE"

IMPORTANT: Do not move on to the 3rd index card immediately after completing the 2nd index card until you are finished with steps 9 and 10:

9. Return to the 1st index card and repeat the *last line* **only** with full sincerity, focus and feeling

10. Return to the 2nd index card and repeat the *last line* **only** with full sincerity, focus and feeling

11. Silently read over the 3rd index card then close your eyes and feel the physical sensation of this desire as being YOUR reality

12. Verbally speak the last line with sincerity, certainty and intention

13. Now, enhance the feeling that captures the essence of this experience while speaking out loud, "IT IS DONE"

IMPORTANT: Do not move on to the 4th index card immediately after completing the 3rd index card until you are finished with steps 14 thru 16:

14. Return to the 1st index card and repeat the *last line* **only** with full sincerity, focus and feeling

15. Return to the 2nd index card and repeat the *last line* **only** with full sincerity, focus and feeling

16. Return to the 3rd index card and repeat the *last line* **only** with full sincerity, focus and feeling

17. Silently read over the 4th index card then close your eyes and feel the physical sensation of this desire as being YOUR reality
18. Verbally speak the last line with sincerity, certainty and intention
19. Now, enhance the feeling that captures the essence of this experience while speaking out loud, "IT IS DONE"

IMPORTANT: Do not move on to the 5th index card immediately after completing the 4th index card until you are finished with steps 20 thru 23:

20. Return to the 1st index card and repeat the *last line* **only** with full sincerity, focus and feeling
21. Return to the 2nd index card and repeat the *last line* **only** with full sincerity, focus and feeling
22. Return to the 3rd index card and repeat the *last line* **only** with full sincerity, focus and feeling
23. Return to the 4th index card and repeat the *last line* **only** with full sincerity, focus and feeling
24. Silently read over the 5th index card then close your eyes and feel the physical sensation of this desire as being YOUR reality
25. Verbally speak the last line with sincerity, certainty and intention
26. Now, enhance the feeling that captures the essence of this experience while speaking out loud, "IT IS DONE"

IMPORTANT: Speak the following 5 statements with the authority of a conscientious co-creator and from a feeling place of deep appreciation:

27. Return to the 1st index card and repeat the *last line* **only** with full sincerity, focus and feeling
28. Return to the 2nd index card and repeat the *last line* **only** with full sincerity, focus and feeling

29. Return to the 3rd index card and repeat the *last line* **only** with full sincerity, focus and feeling

30. Return to the 4th index card and repeat the *last line* **only** with full sincerity, focus and feeling

31. Return to the 5th index card and repeat the *last line* **only** with full sincerity, focus and feeling

Once you are finished following all of the steps from the "Strive for Five System" rip up your index cards or run them through a shredder! You heard me right...there is no reason to repeat this process if you *knew*, before you began, that it would work, the first time around, and doing away with your index cards is a powerful act of faith that all of your requests were instantly received. The wisdom, within, informed you of what your heart-felt desires were, but YOU are always required to ask boldly and believe that it is your birthright to receive your requests.

It has never been about the wisdom, within, being unaware of what you want but always about your willingness to believe in yourself and your dreams. The power, within, is an integral part of you, attached at all times, which is why **it will always be YOU,** who must be completely convinced. Being that getting real results will revolve around your ability to believe, by all means, repeat the process from start to finish, if need be, or reaffirm the last line of each index card with full sincerity, focus and feeling, whenever intuitively instructed.

As a "soon to be" seasoned co-creator, you are also encouraged to design your own unique template and before you know it, you will not even need to follow any pre-set format because you will skillfully start creating, on conscious command. Please be patient with yourself if this system is entirely new to you, and be willing to work this unfamiliar formula for at least 21 days, as experts estimate that this is the approximate amount of time it takes for any new habit to become second nature. Does 3 weeks seem like a long time to go from unfulfilled to skilled? You can take control of the clock by mentally seeing yourself as already being masterful, and enjoying everything that you've summoned with the "Strive for Five System".

I'd like to make one last recommendation before we move on to the final chapter. It would be best to keep all of your designated desires to yourself until after they manifest. There is nothing wrong with sharing everything that excites you, with your support system. However, good natured people love to give advice and this tends to make it much harder to hear or hold onto the perfect plans that are unfolding from within. You can trust that your intuition will advise you on "who" and "who not" to discuss your dreams with, but always be sure to act accordingly. Also know that everything will get easier, with each passing day, and you will eventually be experienced enough to guide your loved ones in bringing their grandest goals, to life.

Generating Rapid Results Right Now

Lose not yourself in a far off time, seize the moment that is thine.
~ Johann Friedrich von Schiller (1759-1805) ~

At this moment, you have gained more experience and expertise, regarding the magical mechanics of manifesting, than more than 90% of the people, destined to cross your path, and who are completely unaware that these procedures exist. Even more exciting is that you are but a few short pages away from embarking on an even bigger adventure, more commonly referred to as *"Destination Co-creation"*. Although we still have some last few loose ends, to tie up, this chapter is officially where "the rubber meets the road". And while there is no way of knowing what path you will take, one thing is for certain: It will lead you to wherever YOU want to go.

Let's make the most of the moment at hand, and take a closer look at all the opportunities that are, at this very moment, readily available to us. It is time to direct our attention away from those doors that have long been closed, and instead, turn our attention to the wide-open doorway to our dreams. It only takes two seconds to do a 180 degree turnaround and this effortless action will make all the difference in regards to the upcoming encounters, events and experiences that we wish to unfold.

It makes no difference if just yesterday, you made a million mistakes or did a thousand things that you are not proud of. There is no need to build a time travel machine, when *today is the day of salvation*, so rise to your feet and hold your head high, regardless of old regrets. The *hands of time* are reaching out to you right now and requesting that you rightfully release every personal or professional relationship and experience that "completed their course" many months ago, but still brings you down, to this day.

The moment of truth has arrived where you are going to have to decide if it is *your will* to beat yourself up further or to be your own best friend, from this day forward. It would be wise to decide the latter because the Universe is living, breathing and listening to every thought we think, whether we are conscious or unconscious of its omnipresent, omniscient and omnipotent operations. In this chapter, I am going to give it everything I've got, to prove that **you are so very valuable** and lead you to the ledge, fully geared up, for the greatest journey of your life!!!

> But even the very hairs of your head are all numbered. Fear not therefore: ye are of more value than many sparrows.
> ~ Luke 12:7 (K.J.V.) ~

Has it ever crossed your mind, how many hundreds of million of other sperm fought for the one and only egg that you successfully seized? You not only *knew* the exact location of the egg but you also managed to beat out a minimum of 180 million other sperm, according to Dr. Lindemann's "Sperm Facts" Article on www2.oakland.edu/biology/lindemann/spermfacts.htm.

Not only are YOU a one-of-a-kind and rightfully won first place to be here but please do not take for granted the fact that over 180 million other soulful sperm competed for chance to be given a body. Set aside ten minutes to contemplate the anatomy of a sperm and then try to dissuade me from believing that these little life forms are not only highly intelligent but immeasurably unique from all of the others.

As strange as it seems, to be discussing sperm, these electrical and microscopic seeds play a most integral role in our physiological makeup, representing our spiritual selves, and seeking expression on earth, by being made manifest into human form. Not a single sculpture or million dollar masterpiece was brought into being by pure accident, but rather, these "creations" were meticulously planned, just as you were meticulously planned! We are told that the very hairs on our head are all numbered, so it goes without saying that everything else that comprises the totality of our being has also been carefully calculated and articulated. You can be certain that YOU are a well-thought-through work of art that began in the mind of the source of all creation, who also just so happens to have the final say as to which human being are admitted into the action park planet earth.

It is so easy to lose sight of our own divinity when surrounded by such magnificence but when we snap back to reality and realize that the universe would have no meaning without us, we awaken to why we are here and how brilliantly, we belong. The mystical and wholly alive mollusk clamshell cleverly conceives, conceals and protects the precious pearl, modeling the apparatus of *your body*, concealing, protecting and sheltering the spiritual spark of wisdom, within *you*.

And Jesus said unto them, Because of your unbelief: for verily I say unto you, if ye have faith as a grain of mustard seed, ye shall say unto this mountain, Remove hence to yonder place; and it shall remove; and nothing shall be impossible unto you.
~ Matthew 17:20 (K.J.V.) ~

All of the darkness in the world does not have the power to snuff out the light of the littlest candle and all I have to say is, "Watch out world!!", when you start tapping into this mustard seed sized spiritual spark, at the center of your being, because *it is actually powerful enough* to move mountains, part seas, oversee the hundreds of billions of galaxies, as well as everything else in existence **and,** *all at the same time!*

The following power points are more valuable than a block of solid gold, so carry around a copy in your wallet and commit them to memory this week:

* **I AM** the beginning and the end *

* **I AM** indubitably implies that it is impossible for me to separate from the life force and love source of all of creation *

* **I AM** activates the spiritual spark that is safely encased in the center of my being *

* The *beginning* is believing and the *end* is receiving *

* **I have** the built-in blueprint to select and expect, like the end-all-be-all entity of everything in existence, therefore, I will stop dancing around the details *

* **I AM** able to call forth things that are not already in existence, and immediately following my definite decision, I know that I must harness my mental forces to project the object of my desire as actually existing physically in my present moment reality *

* I can only be denied the object of my desire *as a reminder* that I need to *remember* to <u>rightfully receive my request</u> **by envisioning my desire as already physically existing in my reality and seeing myself enjoying the possession of my obsession** *

* **I now have no doubt** about what I need to do, as the co-creator that I was born to be, and **I am also well aware** that I beat out millions of others to experience this grand extravaganza called *life*. Therefore, I am honored to be blessed with the wand waving ability to manifest everything that I love *

Here, you have it all!!! **KNOW** that *there is nothing you can't do*, when you put these 8 passages into practice. *The ONLY reason you could possibly fail to receive remarkable results is if you choose not to diligently follow the formula.* As with anything new, the hardest part is to actually start. But once you push past inertia, and get a feel for how intoxicating, as well as liberating it is, in taking back your personal power, your only disappointment will be that you didn't start sooner.

So, say goodbye to sadness, disappointment, and regrets by refusing to dwell on the people that wronged you, or let you down, in the past. Hopefully, they served their purpose, at the time, along with showing you that **you deserve** *people who will not only bring out the best in you but will grow along side of you, for the long haul.* **Don't chase** the flat leavers but instead, **replace** them, **knowing** that the right people WILL walk into your world, the very same week you open your mind to meeting new and magnificent companions. Chances are, that there are plenty of people in your life right now, who could use your undivided love and attention, so put your energy into only those who have proven to be worthy of your affection. You can also start foreseeing new friendships forming, in your mind's eye, should you find yourself missing long lost pals, from the past and sure enough, the most appropriate people will appear on your path, in no time.

It is one thing to think back on good memories from yester-year but it is an absolute waste of our precious thought power, pondering over things that went wrong. As we all get older, our interests and personalities change, and therefore, it is not only natural, but to be expected, that we outgrow some of our old friendships and romantic relationships. The same can be said for the possessions that have disappeared from our lives, as well as the professions that have come and gone, for one reason or another. Old school society suggests that you spend your entire life, working for the same company, until you reach the ripe old age of retirement, **but** *the laws of the universe inspire us to be innovative and creative.*

We were all destined to go from "glory to glory", not "sob story to sob story"….. so, move on with your life and start masterfully manifesting a future, destined to outperform the past, while awakening you to the limitless and glorious opportunities that await you!

Never be afraid to do something new. Remember, amateurs built the ark; professionals built the titanic.
~ Unknown ~

You have what it takes to make a major comeback or discover, for the first time, how it feels, to pull your own strings and lead your life into a whole new level, entrenched with one enchanting experience after another. You need not be afraid that your dues have yet been paid, given that *you have always been entitled to be bold about what you want and expecting of everything you ask for,* simply by following the fail-proof formula that's been set forth, by the source of all creation. Seeking approval and asking for permission are to come to a screeching halt, this very second!!

Walt Disney didn't ask the world if it was a good idea to create Disneyland *because he believed in himself and his dreams.* What would have become of the world, if "The Happiest Place on Earth" had not come into existence, because of doubt and indecisiveness? Now ask yourself this: *If not you, then who, and if not now, then when???* Every expert started out as an amateur but, at this point in time, you are expected to consider yourself the Chief Commanding Officer of Co-Creating because, with all the tools and information you've been given here, you know too much, to turn back now.

You have successfully completed your studies and you should be quite proud of what you have accomplished here. Consider that, as you confidently and enthusiastically prepare to take immediate action, ***right here and right now,*** you will soon give life to your deepest desires, which were once, but wishful thoughts and dreams. Make it your mission to manifest a minimum of 20 meaningful desires, over the next 12 months, by working in batches of 2 to 5, at a time, and always be sure to include the single most important step that almost everyone forgets: **Be ready to receive your result!!!** *Spend* as *little time* as possible, on the believing part of the process, *fast forward* through the middle and *rightfully receive your request*, by seeing yourself, enjoying the possession of your obsession.

HAVE NO FEAR AND STRAP ON YOUR GEAR BECAUSE THIS IS YOUR YEAR!!!

References

Articles:
1. Coon, Robert. "Earth Chakras", © 2001.
<http://www.wyldwytch.com/weavings/articles/pagan_path/pages/earth_chakras.htm>.

2. Lindemann, Dr. Charles B. "Sperm Facts." Michigan: Oakland University; Department of Biological Sciences.
< http://www2.oakland.edu/biology/lindemann>.

3. Simmons, Sandra "How to Become a Millionaire During the Next Depression." 14 Jun. 2008. *EzineArticles.com*. 15 Jun 2009 <http://ezinearticles.com/?How-to-Become-a-Millionaire-During-the-Next-Depression&id=1248222>.

Authors:
Vital, Dr. Joe "Mr. Fire". Texas: Hypnotic Marketing, Inc.
<http://www.mrfire.com/about-joe.html>.

Audios:
Hay, Louise L. "The Power of Your Spoken Word". California: Hay House, Inc.; Unabridged Edition, 2005.

Biblical Verses:
<http://www.biblos.com/>. (See Index)

Books:
1. Covey, Stephen R. "The 7 Habits of Highly Effective People." New York: Free Press; 1st Edition, 1990.

2. Goddard, Neville. "Your Faith is Your Fortune." California: G. & J. Publishing Co., 1941.

Dictionary:
<http://dictionary.reference.com/>. (See Index)

Facts:
1. The Bureau of Engraving and Printing (BEP). "Fun Facts."
<http://www.moneyfactory.gov/document.cfm/18/106>.

2. The Bureau of Engraving and Printing (BEP). "Bureau History."
<http://www.moneyfactory.gov/document.cfm/18/101>.

3. Facts about the Bible. <http://www.allaboutgod.com/bible-facts.htm>.

Story:
NEW THINK: THE USE OF LATERAL THINKING IN THE GENERATION OF NEW IDEAS by EDWARD DE BONO. "The Pebble Story". **Reprinted by permission of BASIC BOOKS, a member of Perseus Books Group.**

Thesaurus:
<http://thesaurus.reference.com/>. (See Index)

Videos:
Stewart, Ben. "Esoteric Agenda." Reality & Illusions, Part 8.
<http://vids.myspace.com/index.cfm?fuseaction=vids.individual&VideoID=42294693>.

Websites:
1. Goldman, Burt. "Quantum Jumping". Nevada: MindValley, LLC, 2009. <http://www.quantumjumping.com>.

2. Hadsell, Helene. "The Winning Sage." Nevada: MindValley, LLC, 2009. <http://www.thewinningsage.com/products>.

Wikipedia:
"Mike the Headless Chicken"
<http://en.wikipedia.org/wiki/Mike_the_Headless_Chicken>.

Index